DESIGNED TO THRIVE

THE FIVE PILLARS OF RETIREMENT PLANNING

A COLLABORATION BY

JAMMIE AVILA AND **KYLE KIRWAN**

At Cornerstone Wealth Management we believe in educating our Las Vegas Community about finances for retirement. That is why we built a large learning center in one of our offices. We hold several public dinner workshops each month that focus on the five pillars of retirement planning. We also host monthly client education workshops so that our clients have the opportunity to learn about the investments they are in. Through education and team-based planning we provide our clients with the elite experience they deserve. We believe this is why our clients trust us with referrals. They want us to be able to help their friends and family the way we helped them. This approach combined with Jammie Avila's leadership since 2009 has helped grow assets to almost 700 million dollars. Jammie and the team look forward to accomplishing their long-term goal of 1 Billion.

No part of this publication may be reproduced, stored in a retrieval system, or transmitted in any form or by any means—electronic, photocopying, recording, or otherwise—without prior written permission, except in the case of brief excerpts in critical reviews and articles. For permission requests, contact the author at info@cornerstonevegas.com

All rights reserved.

Copyright © 2020 Cornerstone Wealth Management

ISBN: 9798670300452

The author disclaims responsibility for adverse effects or consequences from the misapplication or injudicious use of the information contained in this book. Mention of resources and associations does not imply an endorsement.

Cornerstone Wealth Management offers securities through Kalos Capital, Inc. and investment advisory services through Kalos Management, Inc., both at 11525 Park Woods Circle, Alpharetta, Georgia 30005, (678) 356-1100. Cornerstone Wealth Management is not an affiliate or subsidiary of Kalos Capital, Inc. or Kalos Management, Inc.

CONTENTS

PREFACE	*Covid19*	1
FOREWORD		5
CHAPTER ONE	*Who We Are*	9
CHAPTER TWO	*Following a Process*	13
CHAPTER THREE	*Dreaming of Retirement*	21
CHAPTER FOUR	*Building a Solid Fiscal House*	25
CHAPTER FIVE	*Income Planning*	37
CHAPTER SIX	*Investment Planning*	63
CHAPTER SEVEN	*Tax Planning*	77
CHAPTER EIGHT	*Health Care Planning*	91
CHAPTER NINE	*Legacy Planning*	103
CHAPTER TEN	*Choosing a Financial Advisor*	119

PREFACE

When we started writing this book in late 2019, the economy was strong, unemployment was at record lows and the stock market near all-time highs after an unusually long bull-market. Yes, those were halcyon days in the financial services industry. Then, with much fanfare and high expectations, 2020 came roaring in…and things went sideways very quickly. Bushfires in Australia, locust swarms in East Africa, geopolitical tension with Iran and North Korea, protests, and chaos in Hong Kong, an elevated election year, partisan fighting between Democrats and Republicans in the wake of December's impeachment proceedings, and that was just January! Yet despite everything that was happening in this country and around the world, the stock market continued its climb to all-time highs, reaching them on February 12th, 2020.

Enter Covid19. This tiny, invisible, crown-shaped creep ushered in a period of destruction and confusion rarely seen during peacetime; not only in lives lost to the deadly virus, but also in global economic devastation. The US markets experienced the largest one-week declines since 2008, the largest single-day percentage drop since Black Monday of 1987, and eventually an evaporation of trillions of dollars as markets crashed by as much as 30%. Certain stocks in sectors like travel and entertainment saw declines of 80% or more in their value. What we are living through right now is truly a "black swan" event of the likes we have not seen in over a century.

As of writing this preface, we are only a few months into this event, but already are all too familiar with terms like "flattening the curve", "shelter in place" and "social distancing". We know what hydroxychloroquine is and how to properly wear a NIOSH-Approved N95 Filtering Facepiece…we can even make our own protective masks out of a bandana and rubber bands!

Although the economy, society and our way of life have all changed dramatically in a very short time, and even the near future is uncertain, the principles and strategies we discuss in this book remain sound. In fact, living through Covid19 and the wake of chaos it laid down only drives home how important it is to have a financial and retirement plan that can withstand the buffetings of life, be it an unexpected loss of a spouse, a correction/crash in the stock market, or a global pandemic where there is seemingly no safe harbor. By properly constructing your "Cornerstone Retirement Blueprint" (you'll learn about all that in this book), you can rest assured that while the whirlwinds of life swirl about, you know when the tempest subsides, your retirement plan will be intact and life will go on.

Preface

We hope that by the time you read this, Covid19 will be in the past and Corona will once again be a pale lager beer served with a lime wedge. However, if that is not the case, and we are still waist deep in a pandemic, hopefully you will find some nuggets of wisdom from these pages which you can use to find financial peace of mind.

Sincerely,

Jammie Avila and Kyle Kirwan

FOREWORD

You're probably reading this book because you are looking for answers. Answers to questions about retirement, healthcare, investment risk, life expectancy, etc., things you may not have considered until now. Questions like "When can we afford to retire?" or "How do I protect the nest egg I've spent my lifetime building up?"

There may be some anxiety over the amount of your savings: "I've tried as hard as I can to save, but I'm still worried I may outlive my money."

Maybe you're looking for clarity because you feel torn between opposing retirement goals: "My wife and I want to travel in retirement, maybe take a cruise or two each year, but we don't want to spend all of the kids' inheritance…"

Sometimes there's the sinking feeling that, while you know how to invest or budget during your working years, retirement is different. Your income will likely be lower, uncertainties such as medical emergencies, long-term care expense, tax increases—more daunting: "We know we need to cut back on spending and invest more conservatively, but how exactly?"

Coming up with answers to questions like these and more, is what we specialize in at Cornerstone Wealth Management—we are here to help you find solutions specific to your needs.

Before we continue, we would like to give you a little background on us and why we're in a position to write a book about blueprints for retirement. Cornerstone Wealth Management is a full-service financial firm with a concentration in retirement planning. We've been in the Las Vegas valley for over 20 years, with offices in Henderson and Las Vegas, and also serve clients across the United States.

We're writing this book because as much as we enjoy helping those we meet daily in our offices, we know there are many people with whom we may never meet, who need help planning for retirement but don't even know where to begin. If that sounds like you, that's okay. You are not alone. While this book is in no way a comprehensive look at preparing for retirement, and may not speak to your specific circumstances, we hope it will provide some insight on how to lay the foundations of your retirement and develop your own "blueprints," so to speak.

Foreword

We call our five-step planning process the Cornerstone Retirement Blueprint because the approach is like the planning and work that goes into a well-constructed house. All parts must be soundly constructed in and of themselves but must also fit together and function properly as an integrated whole.

The basic ideas and strategies we outline in this book are the culmination of our decades in the industry, our monthly public educational workshops/seminars, personal interviews, and years of broadcasting our message on the airwaves. Our weekly radio show, "The Cornerstone Retirement Hour," is also now available as a podcast where we have candid discussions about strategies and real-life financial issues facing Americans today.

In this book we draw from actual client experiences as the various concepts and strategies are covered. We hope you will find value in the information provided which you can convert into a personal strategy as you begin creating your own foundations for retirement. Let's get started!

CHAPTER ONE

Who We Are

Mike and Brenda arrived at our office with nervous smiles and a canvas bag full of financial statements. As we chatted over coffee, the statements remained in the bag, but we unpacked a little of what brought this couple through our doors.

Mike was a long-time radio station employee. He had a small pension from back in the day when the station offered one and had saved a moderate amount in the company's 401(k) plan. Brenda's background was much more diverse. She was a classically trained teacher who taught for years then operated a private daycare while they raised their three kids and took care of their own parents. Now she was five years into an entrepreneurial role as an early education training consultant. Mike's mother had recently passed away, leaving them a small inheritance from her estate.

We discussed the past, some fond memories, the time spent caring for Mike's mother, and their hopes and dreams for the next few years. Brenda felt that she was just getting into doing what she loved, but she didn't want to feel dependent on her day job to make ends meet. Mike was ready to be finished with a decades-long career but was worried. He was worried about money, worried about how to spend his time, and worried about whether or not they could leave a little for their children the way his parents had done for them.

Underlying all of this were the unspoken questions: Is it enough? Is what we've worked for going to sustain us through our retirement? How can we be sure?

We don't have a crystal ball—there's no way for us to answer with certainty what life will look like for anyone in retirement and beyond. However, helping people like Mike and Brenda nail down their goals and creating a plan to accomplish them is what we do every day for our clients at Cornerstone Wealth Management.

We think about retirement every day, helping people figure out how and when they will retire, and we believe in taking a comprehensive, systematic approach to these issues. Our Cornerstone team includes four partners, knowledgeable advisors, a dedicated and experienced support staff and strategic partnerships with attorneys, CPAs, and Medicare specialists to help our clients accomplish their financial goals.

Chapter One: Who We Are

The *Cornerstone Way* all starts with our mission statement. We think that a mission statement shouldn't be something you craft, hang on the wall, and never look at again. Rather, it should define "who we are, what we do, and why we are in business."

Cornerstone Wealth Management Mission Statement

Our mission is to provide our clients with a foundation for their lives, not only in their investments but in the lifestyle they live. We build our relationships on the premise of lifelong partnerships versus transactional encounters. We believe in being life financial coaches.

At Cornerstone, we believe you should not be alone on this journey (to and through retirement). We will be with you every step of the way.

For us, the activities of financial planning and wealth management are about people, not merely sterile numbers on a spreadsheet. Helping people is what got us into this business, and for over two decades, has made our days interesting and given our lives purpose.

CHAPTER TWO

Following A Process

In this book, we talk about some of the best approaches to general problems. Specifics matter, of course, so we also provide actual case studies on how we have worked to help some of our clients. Perhaps you will see parallels to your personal situation in these examples. Sometimes it's reassuring to know that others have had the same problems you might be facing. All the facts associated with each case are real. However, the names of our clients are changed to protect their privacy.

Let's introduce you to Greta and Luis. When they strolled into Cornerstone Wealth Management's Henderson, NV office for the first time, they had a problem—well, actually, they had multiple problems.

The couple, in their seventies and retired, had relocated to the Las Vegas area from Utah a few years prior to meeting with us. They were not happy with their current financial firm, commonly known in the industry as a "wirehouse," or what some consumers would think of as a mega-brokerage, with offices across the US. This firm had originally appealed to the couple because they thought they could just seamlessly switch their services from the office in Utah to the local Las Vegas branch.

Unfortunately, the couple instantly felt lost and neglected by the mega-firm, getting little in the way of attention and customer service. On top of that, they experienced consistent portfolio losses year after year. Their retirement savings had dwindled from over $500,000 down to about $300,000. Clearly, they attributed this decline to a lack of attention from their financial advisor as the string of losses compounded. What they did not see—yet—was that the portfolio strategy designed for them might have worked in the past but was not suited to their new chapter of life: actual retirement.

It is fairly common for couples like Greta and Luis to come in, looking for something better. They are prime examples of how most clients will benefit from the personalized service an independent firm that specializes in retirement planning can provide over that of an impersonal, one dimensional mega-firm.

Sure, advisors at these large firms have their own arguments: "We have thousands of employees. We can

Chapter Two: Following a Process

handle all your financial needs. If you relocate, we're sure to have an office near you." Yet, that is not what we heard as we were listening to Greta and Luis' story.

They had asked the mega-firm to transfer their account from Utah to Las Vegas, but the company refused, offering up a variety of vague excuses referencing paperwork and transfer problems. Most likely, the fundamental reason for the delays was that their account was simply too small. Large firms with high overhead—big buildings, lots of employees, advertising costs—need to generate larger revenues. Employees have sales goals and quotas to meet. They are reluctant to allocate the requisite time to help the smaller relationships which don't generate the larger commissions and fees.

There was another possibility for the poor customer service and lackluster performance. What advisor in Nevada would want to take on a small account from Utah belonging to a couple who had seen financial disappointment after disappointment? It is not a very attractive undertaking.

Greta and Luis were concerned about the market, and despite some strong overall economic gains, they actually lost money in 2016. As we helped them examine their financial situation, we discovered they were invested in some very aggressive, high-risk positions. They were planning to draw a consistent income from those volatile assets, all while having to communicate their evolving needs and desires to an advisor who wasn't even in their same time zone.

This is a common starting point for those we see in our office. We often start by communicating that our immediate job is, metaphorically speaking, getting them down safely from the top of Mount Everest.

The way we see it, there are two basic phases to retirement: accumulation and distribution. Accumulation is the slow, steady buildup of assets during your working years—say from your early twenties to close to retirement. That's going up the mountain.

Distribution is taking money out—safely—to live on and get to your destination, having the kind of retirement you have dreamed of and not outliving your money. Hopefully, after all is said and done, you'll have something to leave as a legacy for your family or to a charitable cause. That's getting down the mountain.

Climbing Mount Everest also has two phases: ascent and descent. Himalayan Sherpas, some of the best guides in the world, renowned for their mountaineering skills, are responsible for getting you to the top and, just as importantly, back down to basecamp safely. Oft times, the descent is much more dangerous than the climb up. The brief window of good weather that allowed you to get to the summit has likely shut,

Chapter Two: Following a Process

the temperature is dropping, and white-out conditions could blind you at any moment. You're running low on oxygen, your body is starting to shut down from exhaustion, and one wrong step could set off an avalanche or lead to a fatal fall. You must get down, and quickly.

Similarly, when you hit retirement, you have finished the climb up—the accumulation phase. Building up savings is no longer your primary concern; you now need to focus on creating income for the trip down. As life expectancies increase and new medical advances improve our quality of life, that path down the mountain can take years. And there are metaphorical avalanches, storms, and other pitfalls of sorts—medical emergencies, illness, a volatile stock market, political unrest, global pandemics, and other life events. Cornerstone's task is to help you get down the mountain and to your final destination safely.

How does all this relate to Greta and Luis? Despite entering retirement, their portfolio with the previous firm was still stuck in accumulation mode—it was aggressive and took unnecessary risk with their limited funds. Also, they didn't have an adequate approach to the taxes that come with making withdrawals from their portfolio. It was clear that no one had paid attention to their account or made the necessary adjustments to reposition the couple's assets for the "decumulation" part of retirement. Decumulation is essentially the deployment of assets to fund your lifestyle in retirement.

This is where the idea of a comprehensive planning approach comes into play. While we accumulate wealth in our working years, we are conditioned by media pundits, HR managers and financial professionals alike: save, save, save. Put all that money away. Whether it's in a 401(k), private funds, real estate, or what have you, the advice is the same. We come to see our net worth as a pile of assets, culminating in a single number on a spreadsheet, and all set for one goal: growth. Yet, when we switch to decumulation mode, we need our money to do so much more!

Continued growth is still an important part of the plan. No one wants to lose ground to inflation, market losses, taxes, and other erosive forces. But a lot more comes into play at this point in our lives. We need steady, dependable income. We need to address health care and plan for our legacy, and the less we lose through "attrition" from taxes, fees, inflation, and other unseen forces, the more we can keep in our pockets. All these factors mean we must stop thinking of our money as a single pile and instead allocate portions of it to the various financial goals we seek to achieve.

At our firm, the Cornerstone Retirement Blueprint is how we manage to do just that. We cover income, growth, taxes, health care and legacy planning in a systematic way. We aim to build a comprehensive plan that ensures all the pieces of your retirement are working together in a complimentary way. When we see couples like Greta and Luis, it's evident that their previous financial professionals had simply continued to invest their assets for growth, instead of building a strategy that addressed the new goals they had established for their retirement.

Anchored at the core of the Cornerstone way is the valuable service we provide clients with individual, customized, strategy-based planning. We don't have a bloated staff, our overhead is low, and we don't spend money on expensive advertising campaigns. Instead, we pride ourselves on being efficient, taking the time to understand who our clients are as people and what they want to achieve. After all, how can we hope to help our clients reach their final destination and make appropriate lifestyle changes if we don't know what their dreams and goals are, what their lifestyle is like, or what their guiding principles are?

SUMMARY

When approaching retirement, you need to break out of the accumulation mindset and realize you are entering a stage of life where preserving what you have now takes precedence.

Start viewing your assets as more than a lump sum; see each piece as a unique tool to address specific goals.

CHAPTER THREE

Dreaming Of Retirement

"Why are you retiring?"

Occasionally, someone comes into our office and when we first ask this question, they're caught off guard and not quite sure how best to answer.

"I'm not here to talk about that, I'm just here to talk about my investments," they might say.

Another client affronted, replied, "That's personal."

But in our experience, the amount of money and how it's invested isn't very relevant if you don't have a vision of what you want to do with it.

Take Eileen. She came into our office after having gone through a rather drawn out and painful divorce. She sat down with us, arms crossed defensively, and said she had only come in at the urging of her son, and that all she needed was for us to talk about the money. "No personal stuff."

From the way she described it, going forward, she was prepared to live on rice and beans, "making every penny count." The first goal she stated was that she wanted to at least "barely scrape by," and then pass on as much as she could to her son's three daughters. When she talked about them, she lit up, describing what fun she had while taking them to the zoo, exploring art galleries and museums, and sharing experiences in the great outdoors.

Once she opened up and we had worked through some of the more difficult conversations, she shared how proud she was of her son and daughter-in-law. A lawyer and nurse, respectively, they made a decent amount of money and were already well on their way to saving for their kids to go to college and for their own retirements. We asked Eileen if she really believed the best value she could provide to her granddaughters was sacrificing her comfort and lifestyle during retirement in order to pass on the most she could from her estate? When put that way, she agreed that wasn't how she envisioned spending the next few decades. We were able to create a plan where Eileen could draw sufficient income in retirement to allow for quality time with her son and grandchildren and still have a modest amount to leave behind as a legacy.

Chapter Three: Dreaming Of Retirement

It's important to have a well-thought-out strategy for your retirement, but it must fit *your* retirement specifically, focusing on the things that are most important to you. Why plan for expensive European trips if your heart is in a lakeside cabin with the grandkids? Similarly, it's not helpful to plan to live on a shoestring budget if you enjoy entertaining guests and eating out several times a week.

Another good illustration of the importance of knowing what you want when you retire is through the experience of Jacob and Amy. When they came into our office, Amy wouldn't say a word. Jacob kept talking about leaving his job and moving to Colorado to the cabin they vacationed at every year. It took some coaxing—and a few cups of coffee—before Amy finally opened up to us.

"I don't want to move to Colorado. I wanted to ten years ago, but now I actually like my job. And our grandkids are here," she said. "Colorado for a month in the summer is one thing, but I don't want to live there, and I'm certainly not ready to retire." Jacob didn't realize she felt so strongly about the matter. Fortunately, he wasn't put off or offended; Colorado wasn't a big dream for him either. He mistakenly thought it was Amy's dream based on a conversation they'd had a decade earlier. It goes to show that life changes and dreams change, too. Imagine if they had continued to pursue a financial strategy built around a dream that neither of them loved or were fully committed to?

You need to plan for the retirement of your dreams while keeping that same dream rooted firmly in reality.

SUMMARY

When you're ready to meet with a financial professional, be sure to have an idea of how you'd like to spend your time in retirement.

CHAPTER FOUR

Building A Fiscal House

The Cornerstone Retirement Blueprint is a process we developed based on decades of industry experience. We gravitated toward the analogy of building a home because it's tangible and easy to grasp. Especially for those whose eyes glaze over at the mention of obscure financial terms: CDs, IRAs, qualified vs. non-qualified, mutual funds, annuities, ETFs, subordinated debt instruments, convertible bonds, etc.

The image of a house is something we can all envision and have been able to draw since our earliest days doodling in coloring books.

For the reasons mentioned above, we spend quite a bit of time educating our clients about their Fiscal House. If they grasp the concept, then deciding how to construct each section using a diverse array of financial instruments becomes much easier.

At the simplest level, the Fiscal House is an analogy comparing the components of a house—foundation, walls, roof, and fencing—to the various elements of a financial portfolio.

At a more detailed level, the concept is ingrained in those who must implement building a house or a portfolio. The general contractor, engineer, architect and building inspector must be aware of the minimum standards for housing materials and construction methods necessary to withstand the forces of nature and ravages of time. Likewise, the financial advisor, CPA, and estate planning attorney should understand the intricacies of asset management, cyclical economic ebbs and flows, and that investment portfolios need to be designed so that they can withstand forces beyond their, and the clients' control.

Throughout this book, we will quote extensively from a brochure we designed and prepared specifically for our firm to pass out to all our prospective clients. You can find it on our website at www.cornerstonevegas.com.

Let's look at the four major components that go into a Fiscal House:

Chapter Four: Building A Fiscal House

The Foundation

The foundation should be composed of accounts that are stable, safe, and protected from loss. These can include:

- Checking and savings accounts or certificates of deposit that are protected by a federal agency.
- Government bonds, especially those backed by the full faith and credit of the federal government.
- Traditional, fixed, and fixed index annuities—protected by the financial strength and claims-paying ability of the issuing insurance company.
- Certain properly funded cash value life insurance contracts

In shopping for a house, buyers may not even notice the foundation, absent major visible cracks or discoloration. They certainly are not going to be wowed by it, the way the chef in the family might react to granite countertops or stainless-steel Viking appliances. Yet, there is a reason the financial institution loaning the funds necessary to purchase the property insists on hiring someone to crawl around under the house and rigorously inspect the foundation. It is that important! It's what every other component of the edifice is built upon!

One of the wealthiest Americans, financial sage Warren Buffett, sets this cardinal rule of investing: "Don't lose money."

Investing in safe, principal protected assets will help you adhere to Buffet's rule. The ability to generate guaranteed income from a portion of your assets is the foundation of your Fiscal House and the basis for an effective retirement strategy.

The Walls

While the foundation of your Fiscal House is comprised of your safe money, the walls represent the first level of risk in a retirement portfolio. Elements in the walls provide various benefits such as income, tax mitigation and inflation protection. These assets are not quite as risk-free as those in the foundation. Securities commonly placed in the walls include:

- Corporate bonds
- Municipal bonds
- Commodity-type financial instruments such as ownership participation in oil, natural gas, precious metals, farmland, or commercial real estate
- Secured floating rate income

- Private real estate investment trusts, commonly called REITs
- Secured Debt

We may refer to some of the assets in the walls as being "non-correlated" to the market. This means that, by design, they are natural hedges to the roller-coaster ups and downs experienced during volatile stock market fluctuations. We find this reduction in volatility, along with the potential income generated from the underlying investments, helps smooth out the overall portfolio performance.

The Roof

The roof of your Fiscal House represents the highest level of risk your portfolio can tolerate. These securities have the opportunity to grow, but they also can take hits by external forces beyond your control; much in the way a thunderstorm, hail, or exposure to extreme temperatures can damage the roof of your house.

Assets in the roof may include:

- Stocks
- Mutual funds
- Exchange-traded funds (similar to mutual funds but trade like a stock)

- Stock options
- Commodities
- Private Equity

It is important to have a secure foundation and strong walls. Should the roof suffer damage to the risk-based investments it holds, your Fiscal House does not need to crumble completely. Perhaps you may only have to repair some damage to the roof, but your foundation and walls should remain intact and stable.

Fencing

For a home in the physical world, fencing helps keep pets and children safe by preventing them from wandering off. Fencing also discourages intruders from entering the property. In the financial world, your fiscal fence is the insurance that guards your family from portfolio losses that may occur before or after your death.

Life insurance can protect a surviving spouse from a decrease or total loss in income should the sole earner of the household die prematurely. Also, far too often, Social Security and pensions are lost or dramatically reduced when one spouse dies. Life insurance can be structured for a lump-sum payout to counter the loss of the partner's income stream. Some policies can be designed to cover long-term care costs should the surviving spouse needs to move into an assisted care facility.

Although frequently used in the foundation, annuities can also be part of the fencing component. Certain types can provide you and your spouse a lifetime stream of income, backed by an insurance company.

You should now have a good idea as to what goes into the construction of your Fiscal House. At Cornerstone, we try not to overwhelm our clients with too much detail from the financial world. After all, that's why you hire us. You don't need to memorize anatomical charts to undergo surgery or own a complete set of metric flex socket wrenches if the mechanic at an auto shop does the work on your car.

Still, a general understanding of two other concepts may raise your level of confidence in charting the course ahead. They are ***asset allocation*** and ***diversification***.

Asset classes respond differently to economic forces. Stocks may react more violently to an economic downturn than certain types of real estate. One study has found that the choice of assets in a diversified portfolio may determine 88% of the performance over a period of time.

Similarly, not all the financial assets in the same broad asset class react in the same way. Said simply, diversification is the "don't-put-all-your-eggs-in-the-same-basket" maxim.

The Endowment Model

There are countless financial products and the possible combinations and permutations are infinite. Typically, financial advisors will use various favored approaches as they begin shaping a final solution for a client, then make specific adjustments accordingly. There is no need to entirely reinvent the wheel each time at a client's expense and detriment.

One broad approach is the endowment model. When we say endowment, you'd be correct to think Harvard or Yale. Major universities combine donations into an investment pool. The principal in the pool, or endowment, is never supposed to be touched. Only the increase in value from interest, dividends and gain in stock prices is supposed to be harvested, providing scholarships for the university's students or to pay for a new academic wing.

Harvard and Yale know only too well that construction and tuition costs continue to rise. The endowment needs to grow; at the very least, it needs to keep up with inflation. Reasonably steady income from the portfolio is important; however, growth is vital as well. Without it, over time, the endowment will diminish in value, and the income generated will be insufficient to accomplish its objectives.

What happens with an endowment model if there is no income in a particular year or multiple years in a row? That's potentially a nightmare scenario that needs to be considered when constructing an investment portfolio. It must be able to survive the financial equivalent of gale-force winds, torrential rains, or a moderate earthquake.

It is the same with most retirement accounts. The financial advisor must balance the needs for income and growth, tailored to the circumstances of the client, the time horizon for the funds, and their tolerance for taking risks.

The endowment model is one of the broad portfolio design approaches we use in managing our clients' portfolios.

Peter and Diana: Working Hard To Live The Easy Life

After a lifetime of seemingly never-ending hard work, why shouldn't retirement be a time to kick back and let others do the heavy lifting while you spend time relaxing and doing what you love?

Take the case of Peter, seventy-four, and his wife, Diana, seventy. They were the owners of a pest control service, which they recently sold. The early years of business were a struggle, as Peter had to build up the customer base while servicing all the routes on his own. Eventually, he hired an employee to service the routes and continued to increase sales by adding clients in the monthly rotation system.

Peter and Diana worked hard. They were justifiably proud and protective of the business they built from scratch. Then came an offer from a major corporation that was too good to pass up. They took the money from the sale in a lump sum instead of annual installments. Now, instead of living off the revenue from their company, they had to figure out how to generate income from the proceeds, and maybe, just maybe, take some well-earned time off to relax a bit.

Traveling was on the agenda, or maybe even some volunteer work. (*As a side note, Peter recently volunteered at one of the annual charity events hosted by Cornerstone.*) However, that ingrained work ethic and hands-on instinct made letting go of day-to-day management of their finances a bit of a struggle.

The couple came to Cornerstone with a portfolio heavily invested in real estate, too much exposure to the stock market (over $1,500,000 invested in individual stocks and mutual funds), and a goal of drawing $200,000 a year, after tax, while never digging into the principal. Their primary home was valued at around $850,000, and they were still paying off a $250,000 mortgage on the property. They barely used their vacation home in Utah throughout the year, yet they were still servicing a second mortgage on it to the tune of $20,000 a year. They both had accumulated a significant amount in the defined benefit plan they established for the business,

Chapter Four: Building a Fiscal House

and it had performed well over the years. Also, there were some non-retirement investment accounts—remnants of an inheritance Diana received when her mother passed away. Based on their financial situation at that time, their combined investments would require almost a consistent 15% annual return year after year to make it all work. To top it all off, Peter thought his expectations were very realistic and wanted to continue managing it all himself.

Peter and Diana were going to have to face some changes.

To return to our original example of a house blueprint, this was certainly a situation where they had the various parts; however, they weren't all working together as an integrated whole. The amount they were spending for the second home didn't seem like a good usage of funds, and they had little to no assets in the foundation to provide for steady, guaranteed income.

Eventually, they decided to sell the vacation property, thereby reducing their annual expenses. Then using a tax deferral strategy, they rolled the proceeds into an income-producing rental property. Through the reallocation of funds from a top-heavy roof down into the walls and foundation, we were able to provide Peter and Diana with more than adequate income to retire on, and we significantly reduced the risk that was associated with their original portfolio.

By making slight adjustments to current lifestyles or expectations and by taking a systematic approach to their goals, retirees like Peter and Diana can build a more stable, sustainable "house" for their retirement.

SUMMARY

Keep in mind that each investment in your retirement portfolio must work together as part of an integrated whole.

Like a house, your plan will require upkeep—continued tweaks and changes are necessary for your blueprint to continue to reflect your changing lifestyle and circumstances.

CHAPTER FIVE

Income Planning

In the past, you may have sought out the services of a financial advisor because you had concerns about your investments or retirement income.

During your working years and especially in retirement, you need a plan that is custom fit to your life. If a financial professional hasn't taken the time to get to know your specific situation and simply hands you a solution off the rack, chances are the plan is not going to be able to accomplish the goals you've established.

In the fashion world, those with average builds and indiscriminate taste might be happy with choosing a suit or dress off the rack, then having it altered slightly to fit them better. But there is a difference between buying a $200 suit and placing hundreds of thousands or even millions of dollars under a financial professional's protective care.

The guy who stands 6-foot-10 and wears size 18 shoes is probably not going to find anything comfortable in the typical clothing store. Likewise, your financial situation may have an uncommon aspect, something unique that sets you apart from your neighbor, family member or coworker. Do you really want to be shoehorned into an investment vehicle that doesn't fit your needs? That would be like purchasing pants that are two sizes too small or a jacket with sleeves six inches too large.

When planning for income, much of the decision making comes down to your lifestyle. Of course, to keep up with inflation and address any legacy plans you have, you will want money set aside for growth. But your daily needs—the lunch dates, the electricity bill, prescriptions, trips with the grandkids—are things that require a consistent, reliable income stream, one that you don't want to expose to the whims of the market. If the market is down 13% one month, you can't call the power company to declare, "I'm paying 13% less on my electricity bill."

Instead, you will want to establish two things: 1. How much income you will need for regularly occurring expenses; and 2. How much you currently have in consistent, reliable income sources. The income could be from sources such as pensions, Social Security, investment properties, a laddered Treasury bond strategy where you're holding each position to

Chapter Five: Income Planning

term, or a fixed/fixed index annuity. Now compare No. 1 and No. 2. If a shortfall exists, it needs to be addressed, maybe by moving some of your more growth-focused assets to an income-focused investment to bridge the gap.

The following are several scenarios discussing ways to bridge the income gap, as well as some basic income-based strategies retirees have at their disposal.

Dave and Susie: Can We Afford To Retire?

Dave, a lifelong employee of the local power company, walked into the Cornerstone office for the first time, face scorched from the sun where his salt and pepper goatee didn't cover it. He was a big man with a broad smile, pleasant demeanor, and a humble spirit. And he needed help.

For almost a year, Dave had listened diligently to the Cornerstone's Saturday morning radio show while at work, but he never had the confidence to call in to ask for advice. Ultimately, his wife Susie called the show, and after a brief on-air exchange, she set an appointment to come in for a consultation.

Dave was turning sixty-two and had worked at the power company for more than forty years, starting on the job right out of high school. His wife was in her mid-fifties and spent most of her time homeschooling their two children.

Susie was worried. She knew Dave wanted to retire early so he could spend more time with their children. Could their current savings pay for a retirement that might last thirty or more years? What kind of a hit would they take if they started collecting Social Security before reaching full retirement age? These and other questions kept Dave and Susie up at night.

Thus began the first of many meetings with the **Cornerstone Advisor Team**. Sometimes these meetings were late at night because Dave put in twelve-hour days and was just a phone call away from being called into work whenever an emergency power outage occurred.

Our process, the Cornerstone Retirement Blueprint, relies on building sustainable, consistent income as the basis of a stable retirement. For Dave and Susie, the biggest source of retirement funding was going to be the hard-earned $1.5 million Dave had saved up in his company's 401(k) plan – made possible through responsible budgeting and a generous employer match. With those kinds of retirement savings, some might say, "Why worry, what could go wrong?"

Yet, we understood. Income for Dave and Susie was still a concern. Remember, in retirement, they need a stable, reliable source of income, and anything subject to market risk isn't going to be stable or reliable. They were accustomed

Chapter Five: Income Planning

to living on about $90,000 a year—any significant decrease in that amount, their lifestyle would fundamentally have to change.

For many, Social Security is going to be a significant part of their retirement income discussion. You probably know that 62 is the earliest most of us can take Social Security, and that waiting to full retirement age nets a higher monthly check. Delaying benefits for longer increases the monthly payout by 8% each year past FRA (full retirement age) until age seventy.

Many financial advisors recommend waiting until age 70 based on "break-even" charts or waiting until the point at which having a higher monthly check for a shorter period of time provides more money—in total—than being paid for more years but with smaller checks. Yet, break-even charts are generic in nature and don't account for any unique circumstances or needs of the individual recipients.

For one thing, family history plays a significant role. If your grandparents or parents generally had a mortality closer to their seventies, you may not be able to rely on living to a "break-even" age. If your family has a legacy of longevity—that is, you have plenty of nonagenarians or centenarians in the family tree—you might consider taking Social Security later. Also, it's important to remember Social Security is not inheritable. Your spouse may get your monthly benefit check upon your death if it is higher than theirs, but beyond that, your kids and grandkids won't receive those benefits. This is an important point to consider when determining when and how to take your Social Security. Another consideration is whether you should take Social Security income earlier and live off that income, therefore allowing you to preserve your own hard-earned and inheritable assets?

These questions are some that are quite formative to discuss with a financial professional who can give you insights into the various Social Security filing status options as well as the impact they can have on the rest of your strategies. For instance, one thing we discuss with families in a similar position to Dave and Susie's is that Social Security has a minor child provision. It pays additional benefits to a retiree until the children turn "of age," or eighteen (nineteen if he or she is still a full-time high school student).

A strategy like that, implemented for someone in Dave and Susie's situation, could net more than $80,000 because both children would give them close to four years of qualifying for an extra $1,000 per month per child.

At Cornerstone, we have the experience and specialized software to enter various "what-if" scenarios, that include not just investment positions and market scenarios, but also

Chapter Five: Income Planning

Social Security filing strategies and how they interplay with your other assets. Social Security with dependent children, divorced spouses, widowed spouses or for any number of scenarios, can all have different strategies and filing consequences. And each strategy will affect the way you withdraw from your other assets, create reliable income, and pay your taxes.

Jim and Etta: Pioneering A 401(k) Fix In Nevada

Nevada is a pioneer state, comprised of frighteningly long stretches of waterless desert that wagons had to cross on their way to California or to capitalize on our state's own "silver rush" of 1859. This was a century before modern air conditioning, when gambling, lax liquor laws, and easy divorce requirements lured people to head out west and plant their roots in the dusty, scorched earth of the southwest.

We're on the downside of almost two centuries separating us from those hearty pioneers, but Cornerstone Wealth Management is still pioneering new strategies and techniques in the financial space. Here's an example.

Jim and Etta were in their mid-fifties when we met them, still happily married after thirty years together. She worked in an attorney's office; he was employed by a technology company.

One of them had a 401(k) plan with hundreds of thousands of dollars in it. That was the good news.

They were getting close to retirement. Jim and Etta remembered the economic crisis of 2008, and they were worried about losing a large portion of their tax-sheltered portfolio as they approached retirement. They feared that a financial downturn would hit just when they needed to draw on their retirement accounts. Despite the benefits of participating in the company's retirement plan, they could also see some flaws in a 401(k) program. That was the bad news.

As pensions continue to decline around the country, we see more couples with 401(k)s as their primary source of retirement assets. Pensions are expensive to maintain and are perceived as too risky for even large corporations. Now 401(k)s and IRAs are the vehicles most people are using to prepare for retirement. You're probably well-acquainted with the set up: Deductions from employee paychecks are put into tax shelters. In a traditional 401(k), the money, if invested prudently, can grow tax deferred over time. On the downside, there are no guarantees against loss. The employee assumes all the investment risk and the tax burden grows along with the account balance.

Chapter Five: Income Planning

These types of qualified employer-sponsored retirement plans help employees efficiently accumulate money for retirement; however, when the time comes for taking distributions, they aren't quite as effective. There are restrictions placed on taking money out of qualified plans. For example, participants still working who are younger than 59 1/2 generally cannot withdraw money without paying hefty penalties.

These restrictions can be a good thing as they tend to enforce discipline on many who might be tempted to pull money out for everyday expenses. However, this locked-in feature can put people in their 50s at a severe disadvantage. Many have built up a sizable amount in their retirement accounts. What options do they have if the economy becomes unpredictable or the stock market tanks?

The employer is responsible for choosing the 401(k)-plan administrator, and the employee has no say in the matter. If the administrator is a large financial firm, there may be many choices on how the employee can invest his or her money. For companies signed up with smaller firms, there may be far fewer options to flee should the market take a bearish turn. During volatile times, the only option may be to move their money to cash or put it in a stable mutual fund if one is offered.

Now, for those younger than 59 ½ who want to find a way to place some of the money in a less restrictive retirement vehicle, careful research and a bit of pioneering have yielded some potential options which we will discuss.

Although divorce can often be a difficult and painful time in a person's life, one silver lining is the fact that there is an escape clause from the locked-in feature of 401(k)s for couples going through a divorce. Money will separate into two halves. The fancy name for the process is a Qualified Domestic Order. The judge typically requires a QUDRO before sending it to the administrator of the company's plan and directing that the money be separated.

Here's the loophole Cornerstone discovered: Nowhere in a QUDRO does it say a divorce is necessary for the separation of the property. So, if you have a couple with a strong marriage and they want a good portion—not all—of their money removed so they can have access, the QUDRO might be the vehicle.

Before Cornerstone began to use this strategy, it had been done in other states, but never in Nevada. Granted, this is only a viable option when working with a couple who has a strong marriage and who isn't concerned that one of the parties will run off with their "half" in the thirty or so days during the property separation. This separation of funds

Chapter Five: Income Planning

allows one portion to stay invested as-is while moving the other portion to different, potentially less risky allocations, such as bonds or perhaps annuities.

Many couples in their mid-50s are still scrambling to build up their savings for retirement. A couple in a similar situation to Jim and Etta, as mentioned earlier, may be well on their way to reaching their retirement goals and want to protect some of what they have while allowing another portion to grow in investments tied to the stock market.

Is this a complicated way to achieve that? Yes. However, the money saved is *theirs*, and this strategy can allow for more investment options. This is especially true when the company 401(k) limits investments and doesn't have conservative options, such as bond funds, annuities, or life-stage/target-date funds, which rebalance as the participant gets closer to retirement.

For many, company-sponsored retirement plans are something you set up then forget about. In our experience though, it pays to pay attention to your 401(k) plan, at least occasionally, especially when retirement is near. The investment risk and the responsibility of managing such an account fall squarely upon the employee.

Let's look at a couple more real-life examples of Cornerstone clients who faced some difficult decisions when it came time for income planning in retirement. Maybe you might find some parallels to your own situation.

Chuck's Dilemma: Lump Sum Or Annuity

Chuck is that rare individual who spent his entire career, all forty-one years, working for the same telecommunications company.

He was not an executive, just a hard-working, blue-collar employee on an hourly wage, a single father of four who put his head down, did his job well, and was "Mr. Reliable" for more than four decades.

When he first met with an advisor at Cornerstone, he was on the verge of retirement—or maybe not. Chuck was scared that he did not have enough savings for an expected 20-30+ years in retirement based on family longevity. What to do: a monthly pension check from his employer or a lump sum payment upfront? This was not the type of decision he was used to making.

It is, however, a situation we often see at Cornerstone. This year alone, we had six people come to us who each received buyouts of more than $500,000. These were blue-collar workers, putting in their forty-hour weeks, and they never had to worry about investing because they were going to have a monthly pension check from their employers.

Chapter Five: Income Planning

Then came the lump-sum buyout surprise, and they needed someone to help them through the process.

Chuck was divorced and had successfully raised four kids on his own. Now, as an empty nester, he liked to spend his free time in the outdoors fishing, hiking and relaxing. His dad was ninety years old, so Chuck assumed he was also looking at a long retirement, despite some minor issues with diabetes.

Divorces can be traumatic, both emotionally and financially, and Chuck's was no exception. He had filed for bankruptcy three years prior to meeting with us, in part because of the divorce expenses and because he did not have enough equity in their house to buy out his wife. Chuck and his former wife were among the casualties of the mortgage meltdown in 2007-2008, and the adverse effects were still being felt years later.

Retirement was a chance for a new chapter in life, and Chuck was seeking a rebirth of sorts. He had put in his time for four decades, and now he was looking forward to pursuing the more enjoyable things in life. But could he afford to retire, particularly if he lived as long as his father? What's more, just days after retiring, he was faced with the difficult choice between receiving a fixed monthly payment for the rest of his life or taking a lump-sum payout from his retirement account. It's an irreversible choice, and who knows what the future will bring?

Cornerstone had plenty of work to do for Chuck. Would our first task of business be helping Chuck with "The Decision?"

No. That's a decision a client must ultimately make on their own, but only after comparing all the options. What Cornerstone does is thoroughly research the situation then present the numbers and facts to our clients. For Chuck, we presented two scenarios and the facts around both options. Once Chuck decided what course of action he felt most confident about, Cornerstone took over and implemented the plan.

This may sound obvious, but the decision on how best to take income in retirement will change depending on the circumstances. If Chuck were single with no grown children, for instance, and just wanted the highest income possible, he probably would have chosen the monthly pension check. Or, if he were married with no offspring, he might choose a monthly check for a lesser amount with a survivor benefit.

With a lump-sum payment rolled into a tax-sheltered Individual Retirement Account, he could move the money around or adjust the draw, if necessary. If he took a monthly pension check (essentially a form of annuity) and died early,

Chapter Five: Income Planning

the company would keep the rest of the pension money. There would be no death benefit. He had worked forty-one years for that pension money, and in the event of a premature death, he would be giving it back to the company—that wasn't what he wanted. Furthermore, if his health or lifestyle changed, he would not have the freedom or the flexibility to alter his income benefit to accommodate the new normal.

Ultimately, it's just a numbers game between different choices. Yet, it is so much more.

The allure of security beckons with the monthly check option. Could that be a trap? Chuck was 66 with some minor health issues. What happens if his health starts failing and he needs long-term care? Would his monthly income be sufficient? Or, what if a future medical advance makes a new experimental treatment possible, but he needs to come up with $50,000 out of pocket for the procedure. Where is he going to pull that amount from? Often with married couples, we see one spouse take care of the other when they suffer illness later in life. But for someone who is single, that may not be an option to delay the onset of long-term care costs.

For someone like Chuck, who wanted to exercise control over part of his assets but still have a consistent paycheck, he could take the pension as a lump sum and then convert some of it into an annuity. The annuity would pay a consistent pension-like check each month and still allow him the freedom to invest the rest without concern for how stock market movements might adversely affect his income.

The Curious Case of Ms. Browne

Ms. Browne is a special case to us. We met her in the throes of the "*Great Recession*" at one of our workshops, and she wanted to schedule an appointment at her home as soon as possible. We set something up for the next day, and when she answered the door, it was obvious from the look on her face that she was worried.

Ms. Browne's concerns were fairly common among many of the people we met with during that terrible economic time. We had just come off 2008—by far the worst market correction since the Great Depression. There was a lot of financial uncertainty, and anyone who had their nest egg invested in stocks, mutual funds, ETFs, etc., was dealing with serious losses.

At the start of any consultation, we normally like to find out a little about the prospective clients. Where are they from? What did they do for a living? How old are they? Are they married? Are there other dependents? Often, during a consultation, a time comes when it makes more sense to stop asking questions and just listen instead to what the client has to say.

Chapter Five: Income Planning

Ms. Browne began telling her story and why she wanted an appointment with Cornerstone. She was 71 years old and had been divorced for a long time. She worked for a major corporation for more than thirty years, regularly contributing to her company 401(k) account with a match from her employer.

On the cusp of retirement, she had amassed almost $1 million in this tax-deferred account. With confidence, she decided to retire in late 2007. Her 401(k) had slowly come back to life after the tech bubble and the effects of 9/11 nearly wiped her out in 2001. But her advisor had told her not to panic and that the stock market would come back. She was right.

After five years of market recovery from 2003 through 2007, she had recouped all her losses and more, thanks to her continued 401(k) contributions and company match. Her broker had told her that she would be able to take 7% withdrawals from her million-dollar account each year and that her principal would remain the same. She had assured her that this was a standard, safe withdrawal rate, and she would never have to worry about running out of money.

It was easy to tell by looking at her home and the car she drove that this was the retirement for which she had always hoped. She was taking close to $70,000 a year from her 401(k) account and had an additional $20,000 a year coming from "Uncle Sam" through Social Security. With this $90,000 a year in income, she could meet all her housing, transportation, and other expenses. She even had enough money to take a couple of trips a year with family and friends. Life was great.

Then something happened that was worse than what she had experienced in 2001 and 2002—the real estate bubble of 2008. In Las Vegas, there was record devaluation in the housing market. Many homeowners saw their real estate values cut in half after all was said and done. Few were spared from the real estate correction.

Timing is everything. If you had bought a home in 2004-07, chances are you were completely upside down on your mortgage by the end of 2008. If that had been the extent of the bad news, Ms. Browne probably could have lived with it. She was upside down on her mortgage, but with $90,000 in annual income, she could still easily make the payments.

Unfortunately, she was dealt a double blow that same year. Not only had her home value plunged, but each month when her brokerage statements arrived, she was horrified as the balance kept falling. Worried, she would call her broker and ask for guidance. On the rare occasion when she did

Chapter Five: Income Planning

answer, she kept saying the same thing each time: "Don't worry, the market will come back."

She had faith in that mantra as firsthand experience from previous bull markets and corrections proved that her investments would bounce back. So, for the rest of the year, she tried not to worry and ignored the statements that arrived in the mail. By the end of 2008, her 401(k) account was down to $550,000. She could not believe it!

How would she ever get back the money she had lost? She no longer worked, and there were no contributions or employer matches to replenish her investment account.

Then she got the dreaded phone call from her broker. She informed her that if she did not want to outlive her money, she needed to reduce her annual withdrawals from 7% down to 3-4% of her account value each year. What was once a healthy income of $70,000 a year from her investments was now a measly draw of $20,000. Her Social Security check was the same, but she had gone from $90,000 a year to $40,000 in total income. That was not enough to meet her financial obligations or pay for the standard of living she had grown accustomed to the past few years. Maintaining her $70,000 income stream from her retirement account wasn't an option since what was once a 7% withdrawal rate (pretty aggressive by any measure) was now over a 12% rate based on her reduced account balance.

The broker had made some major mistakes in retirement planning for Ms. Browne.

Let's tackle the broker's first downfall: asset allocation during the retirement years.

Brokers generally do a great job during their clients' working years—which we referred to earlier as the accumulation phase. The problem is that when their clients start the distribution phase, brokers usually continue with the same asset allocation they had used in the capital accumulation phase. In other words, they keep a high percentage of the portfolio in stocks and mutual funds.

In the case of Ms. Browne, her broker had her 100% invested in equity mutual funds. Aside from the rare exception, we believe it is irresponsible to have a 69-year-old who had just retired, invested in a portfolio allocation carrying that much risk. Unfortunately, she was extremely vulnerable to a downturn in the market, and the downturn came. In 2008 when the stock market dropped by more than 40%, Ms. Browne was completely exposed and didn't have any positions or investments that helped soften the financial blow.

Chapter Five: Income Planning

There is a simple system called the Rule of 100 that Cornerstone adheres to with many of our clients. If most financial advisors used systems like this in their planning, it would save their clients a lot of heartache. The Rule of 100 is particularly valuable for the guidance it provides during the retirement years.

The rule takes into consideration your age and investment time horizon to better define your risk tolerance. It uses your age as a baseline in the calculation to appropriately allocate your portfolio. Subtract your age from 100. That provides an immediate snapshot of what percentage of your retirement assets should be in the market (at risk) and what percentage should be in safe money alternatives. This strategy will reduce your exposure to market risk and volatile market swings that most people experienced in 2008.

For example, a 69-year-old client such as Ms. Browne had $1 million saved for retirement. Subtract 69 from 100 to get 31. In this illustration, the client should have no more than 31%, or $310,000, of their assets at risk in stocks. That leaves 69%, or $690,000 of the assets, to allocate to less risky alternatives.

The broker's second downfall was income planning.

She had assumed that since the stock market had rebounded after the tech bubble, it was appropriate to tell her client she could take a 7% withdrawal during her lifetime and not run the risk of running out of money. Any time you are in an account that is exposed to risk, you cannot guarantee your money will last your lifetime.

In 1994, William Bengen published a paper in the *Journal of Financial Planning* that had a big impact on retirement income planning. Bengen, in what was titled "Determining Withdrawal Rates Using Historical Data," looked at actual stock market returns and retirement scenarios over the previous 75 years.

He concluded that retirees who draw down no more than 4% of their portfolios every year stand a good chance their money will outlive them. Retirees who draw 5% a year, however, run a 30% chance of jeopardizing their nest egg. Those who draw 6 to 7% have a much greater risk of running out of funds in their lifetime.

Ibbotson Associates, an affiliate of Morningstar Inc., found in a 2006 study that systematic withdrawals of more than 3 to 4% annually can be problematic. Based on historical rates of return, the study found that with a balanced stock and bond mix, a 7% annual withdrawal could deplete in nine years. At a 5% withdrawal rate, the money has a good chance of lasting about 22 years. Cut that to 4% or less to make the portfolio last at least 30 years.

Chapter Five: Income Planning

Now in defense of Ms. Browne's broker, she did not know that a 2008-style event was looming in the future. The lesson to be learned is that if you want predictable income during retirement, you should never have that income tied to an account that is taking inappropriate amounts of risk.

Unfortunately, there was nothing Cornerstone could do to help Ms. Browne immediately recoup her losses. The damage had been done. If we had met Ms. Browne back when she retired, we would have done things differently. However, we were able to stabilize her portfolio and restructure some other assets, allowing time for her investments to recover.

Now we'd like to step out into the theoretical. We cannot say with any degree of certainty what Ms. Browne's outcomes would have been with our firm. Yet, we will use her case to put our income planning strategies to the test. If we could travel back in time, this is how we might have approached her situation and needs.

For starters, we may have used a fixed income or hybrid annuity for a portion of the portfolio due to several advantages associated with those products. A hybrid annuity provides a guaranteed income that the client can never outlive. Using the Rule of 100, when Ms. Browne retired at age 69, we might have put 69% or $690,000 in a hybrid annuity for guaranteed lifetime income. She could have taken a guaranteed withdrawal of 5.9% or $40,000 a year for the rest of her life. She could then invest the remaining 31% or $310,000 into an intelligently designed brokerage account from which she could withdraw some income and still have the potential for future growth.

Taking 4% a year out of the brokerage account would have provided an additional $12,000 a year. Her income from her combined portfolio would have been $52,000 a year. Although less than the $70,000 a year she was taking before, it would have been much more predictable and realistic.

Another advantage of a hybrid annuity is that some have a long-term care feature built into the contract. If a client's health changes in the future, and he or she is unable to perform at least two of six daily living requirements, the client qualifies for the "home health care doubler." Those six daily living requirements are bathing, dressing, eating, transferring, continence, and toileting. The doubler provision means their income from the annuity can double for up to five years. In Ms. Browne's case, it would have taken her income from $40,000 a year to $80,000 if she suffered a major negative change in her health. The money can go toward receiving care and treatment in her home, and there is no requirement that the individual check into a long-term care facility.

Chapter Five: Income Planning

What happens if the client does not need income right away? Deferring withdrawals allows the account to grow, turning into greater income down the road.

In our initial consultations with prospective clients, Cornerstone always asks whether they want their future income to be *"maybe"* income or *"guaranteed lifetime"* income. After hearing Ms. Browne's story, we think you understand why.

SUMMARY

Know how much your lifestyle costs.

Work with a professional who is knowledgeable of Social Security, pensions, annuities, and other income sources that are steady and reliable.

Cover your necessary lifestyle expenses in a steady paycheck that will come each month no matter what market conditions arise.

CHAPTER SIX

Investment Planning

Life does not come with guarantees. The shift to retirement is much the same. Forget for a moment, the financial aspects. There are the unknowns of how long we will live and how long we can stay healthy. These unknowns threaten to overwhelm what any individual or couple can do in financial planning, especially those without professional training or a blueprint to follow.

We may look forward to our idealized visions of retirement where we have freedom from an employer's demands and rigid schedules. In retirement we can choose to travel, take up some new hobbies, volunteer, or do absolutely nothing. Yet, too often retirement leads to a clash between dreams and reality. Travel is an escape, but it also takes us away from friends, our roots, our home. Sometimes, when you're halfway around the globe, surrounded by people who speak a foreign language, eat different food and enjoy a different lifestyle, you can become—well, lonely.

Or consider the stay-at-homes. Freedom from work means we can finally take on those tasks we never seemed to get around to. Then comes the realization: How often can you clean out the garage or paint the eaves? Quality time with the spouse sounds idyllic. Going from the forced separation of ten-hour workdays to constant togetherness, however, can be an abrupt journey from one extreme to another.

What about the financial guarantee of the company pension that we labored so long for? For many in the work force it has disappeared, a traditional benefit that ultimately proved too costly for companies to continue. For others, such as the self-employed, the pension never existed in the first place.

Replacing the pension, employees may have Individual Retirement Accounts or 401(k) plans with a partial employer match. Self-employed entrepreneurs or professionals may have a version called SEP IRAs (Simplified Employee Pension Individual Retirement Accounts). As discussed earlier, these retirement programs are forms of incentivized saving. They are tax shelters, typically deferring federal and state taxes until money is withdrawn, preferably in the golden years. In the end, there may be money set aside for retirement,

Chapter Six: Investment Planning

but no guarantees as to how much or how to create a steady stream of income when the paychecks end.

For the financial advisor and client, many challenges exist such as how to remove money gradually from a tax-sheltered account to avoid a precipitous tax bill? How to create a stream of income so that the money coming in each month is predictable? Even when you are decades away from retirement, there are factors to consider. Suppose your retirement is 20+ years away, what is an appropriate investment strategy if your current stockpile of savings and projected Social Security are insufficient?

The stock market cannot be counted on to provide a steady flow of money in retirement or to even guarantee that there will not be stomach-turning losses. Yet, investing in the market is also one of the best ways to keep up and outpace inflation. In your accumulation years, you need to keep your assets moving in a positive direction, even if that journey upward takes decades while riding a roller coaster of ups and downs. So how can a retiree balance these needs for growth, consistency, and security?

If you have been following the Cornerstone Retirement Blueprint, you'll have already built a solid foundation of income, so you know your day-to-day expenses are taken care of. The next step in the process is to take a look at what assets are still available and determine where best to put them. What you don't need for daily expenses or emergency liquidity becomes your growth money. This is the money you can prudently invest in the previously mentioned "walls" and/or "roof" of your fiscal house.

For some retirees, their investment strategy will always look more conservative—that's just who they are. For others, the knowledge that daily expenses and bills are covered by their income plan gives them the ability to be a bit more aggressive and invest a portion of their assets with an attitude closer to that of their working years.

Regardless of how "aggressive" or "conservative" you feel, diversification should always be an important part of your strategy, spreading your dollars among not only different investments, but different asset classes too. We've discussed some of the various tools that can be selected from the toolbox—mutual funds, exchange-traded funds, individual blue-chip stocks, fixed income, alternatives, real estate and more.

Staying consistent with the idea of efficiency in mind, your investments should be in line with your risk tolerance, time horizon, liquidity needs and you should always be cognizant of the impact from fees and taxes.

Chapter Six: Investment Planning

Kent: Finding a Way to Peace of Mind

Here is the story of Kent, a client who, while better off than most, never had any expectation of ever receiving a pension.

Kent is a dentist—actually, a periodontist who specializes in implants. Recently single with a divorce shrinking in the rear-view mirror, Kent was enjoying the twilight of his career, having just sold his practice. Still, he enjoyed his work and put in about fifteen hours a week at the office. At seventy-one, he planned to continue helping people with their dental health for at least another four years before putting away his periodontal probes for good.

We understand that dentists, doctors, and lawyers put in extra years of costly education, complete grueling internships and are successful because of their exceptional talents, experience, and work ethic. They tend to be compensated accordingly. Kent's down-to-earth demeanor, however, wouldn't make you think that he once earned in excess of $400,000 a year. Even in a reduced role, he brought in about half that amount.

He had a zest for life and expected to be around for a long, long time. Kent's mother was 98 years old and lived in another state. He would check on her well-being daily and hoped to become a centenarian like his mother was soon to be, perhaps even reaching 105!

Dentists tend to be on their feet much of the day, so Kent's leisure passion seemed almost ironic: he's a marathon runner. He ran them often and in various locations, although he wisely avoided any races in Vegas during July and August. He planned to continue his participation in marathons after retirement and was preparing for one of the oldest marathons in the United States, the Rock-N-Roll Las Vegas Marathon.

Kent was someone who believed in giving back, always active in his church and community activities, and was involved in the Boy Scouts of America.

Kent was a pioneer. In the days when Downtown Las Vegas and The Strip were rising up from the dusty Vegas valley, and modern residential air conditioning helped lead to the creation of the great cities of the Southwest, Kent set up his practice. He was among the first periodontists in the Las Vegas Valley. He would grow with the times as the decades brought to his profession better materials, improved techniques, and the amazing precision and power of the personal computer. Even though Kent had a successful career, accumulating more than $1 million in his retirement account, when he first approached Cornerstone, he was still uncertain about his future and on the quest for long-term financial security.

When he came to our office six years ago, he was looking for help. He wanted to know whom he could trust with his

Chapter Six: Investment Planning

financial future. And he wanted to learn more about the whole retirement process.

The "nemesis" in this story is a common one: Kent had no safety net, no guaranteed pension, no predictable income stream that would cover his basic needs after he stopped working. Sure, he had more than $1 million in assets, but numbers are relative. When you're accustomed to earning $400,000 to $500,000 a year, you don't want your income to be decimated just because you retired.

Like so many people, the biggest problem for Kent was the unknown. When people retire, they want to retire with peace of mind and with security. They don't want to wake up at 4AM in the morning, unable to sleep, turn on CNBC and watch the market—and their investments—tumble.

Just because someone didn't spend twenty, thirty, or forty years working for a company that offers a pension, doesn't mean they aren't able to have the same peace of mind that a pension provides. Knowing that you have a check coming to your mailbox every month for the rest of your life—regardless of what happens to the company you worked for, regardless of what happens to the stock market—is the ultimate peace of mind.

For someone like Kent, we would begin by setting up an income stream, likely using a combination of annuities and some stocks that reliably pay dividends. We'd examine sources like Social Security and his investments for tax efficiency. But once we've established a reliable income stream, there's no reason someone like Kent shouldn't be able to invest some of his other assets in the market.

By nailing down income first, we can be more aggressive with a portion of a client's portfolio without them worrying that they won't have enough money to pay their bills. For someone who has long life expectancy in their family history like Kent, they will want to have some aggressive investments with a longer time horizon to at least keep up with (and hopefully beat) inflation. If inflation holds steady at its historical average (around 3.2%) then to maintain the purchasing power of $200,000 today you would need to grow that amount to $413,824 over thirty years. For Kent, if he lives beyond age one hundred, a 30 plus year retirement could be his reality. Having investments set aside to take on inflation is a must when you are potentially looking at decades in retirement.

Now, the exact numbers in this example aren't as important as the principles involved. Everyone, regardless of where they start on the economic scale, wants more security and stability. Stability and predictability are preferable over having all your money invested in the market and hoping that everything turns out okay. That's just gambling. Yet, without maintaining at least a portion of your portfolio invested in equities, you could slowly lose purchasing power as inflation eats away at your nest egg.

Dorothy: A Prescription For An Overly Risky Portfolio

Risk and reward tend to go hand in hand when it comes to investments. Usually, the higher the potential reward, the higher the risk of loss. The amount of risk someone is willing to accept is called their "risk tolerance". Some people are afraid to accept any risk. Risk tolerance tends to be a function of one's personality, goals, time horizon, experience, and of course, financial situation. Quite frequently, someone preparing for retirement may not know the person they see in the mirror as well as they think they do.

We often ask our clients about their risk tolerance—meaning are they willing to take a degree of additional risk for a chance at more income? Or would they prefer to be able to sleep better at night and accept a lower level of income with the reduction in risk?

Frequently the answer is, "I don't like risk. Let's avoid risky investments and protect the nest egg." That may be the answer now, however, a few years later, their investments might tell a different story.

Take, for instance, Dorothy. She had a big problem, and it took a number of years for her to even realize it. And then quite some time and effort after that to figure out a solution.

By age 50, she retired as a pharmacist after she sold her practice for $3.2 million. Years prior to selling her business, she and her husband had divorced. So as a single woman, she started off her retirement with ample funds, but the money needed to last for thirty to thirty-five years, or maybe even longer.

Dorothy was sweet and humble. Few would guess that she was a multi-millionaire.

Her first financial advisor invested her heavily into stocks, and unfortunately, the market did not cooperate. By 58, her portfolio had shrunk to the point where she felt like she needed to go back to work. The losses weren't so extreme that she panicked, but she did want to replenish the coffers. Besides, she missed helping people as a pharmacist and thought it would be mentally and emotionally beneficial for her to get back behind the medicine counter.

Although she was in retirement for less than a decade, the pharmacy industry had changed quite a bit during her time away. No longer were they located in the corner drug store on Main Street USA. Now they were found in supermarkets and strip malls. They were even in those Big Box wholesale/

Chapter Six: Investment Planning

retail outlets, the kind that carry everything from cat food to computers. Dorothy landed a part-time job with one such warehouse chain and found the work invigorating. She especially enjoyed being freed from the responsibilities of management and meeting a payroll like she had to do when running her own company.

On the weekends while catching up on housecleaning, Dorothy frequently found herself listening to our Saturday morning radio show "The Cornerstone Retirement Hour," the predecessor of our current podcast. She listened for about six months before finally calling the show, mostly out of curiosity.

Why did she call? Because she was concerned about the performance of her investments, the high fees she was paying to her advisor, and the fact that she just found out the alternative minimum tax had been triggered.

Cornerstone met with her for the first time in 2015. We discovered that all her money had been put in just one asset class: US domestic stocks. The market reversal in 2008 and 2009 had slashed her portfolio from $3.5 million to $2.1 million. Her former advisor told her to stay the course, and she did. In seven years, the portfolio rebounded to $3.1 million, still short of the original $3.5 million she started with.

Cornerstone researched Dorothy's historical portfolio makeup and found plenty of holes. As mentioned before, the most glaring misstep was having all her assets invested in domestic stocks. This did not make sense. She was paying roughly $50,000 in portfolio management fees, and due to her $92,000 income as a pharmacist, she was also paying $32,000 in taxes because of the alternative minimum tax.

When she retired the first time, not having an adequate income in the foundation also hobbled her investment performance. She wasn't comfortable trying to grow her account because she needed to protect it for income purposes. Then, when she went back to work, her financial professional never adjusted the allocation in her portfolio to account for the change in her income and tax circumstances.

This is one of the main reasons we use the Cornerstone Retirement Blueprint at our firm—we understand that plans change. Having a mechanism in place to help decide what those changes mean and how they affect the investment strategy is crucial to achieving our clients' financial objectives.

We see people like Dorothy who aren't invested in a way that would allow for growth but also aren't positioned for income either. This is a bad combination leading to inefficient and stagnant portfolios. That's why it's so important to segregate the various parts of your portfolio, each to suit specific needs in accomplishing your overall individual goals and purpose.

SUMMARY

If you have established your income stream, identify the goals you have for the remaining investments. Moderate Growth? Aggressive Growth? Outpace inflation?

Be sure the risks you are taking align with your goals and your risk tolerance.

Diversification is the name of the game—be sure your eggs are not all in the same risk-structured or tax-treatment basket. Diversify across asset classes, not just within the stock/equity universe.

CHAPTER SEVEN

Tax Planning

Baby boomers, the generation born between 1946 and 1965, are generally prolific savers, and they understand that 401(k) retirement plans are a great vehicle to do just that. Between tax-sheltered growth, automatic paycheck deductions, and sometimes even employer-matched contributions, what's not to like?

Once 76.4-million strong, the Boomers are retiring at an estimated clip of over 10,000 every day. Those fortunate enough to participate in employer-sponsored plans are grateful. They realize that this formal program of regular, incentivized savings has allowed them to amass much more than they could have done on their own.

One aspect of these plans that's not so great is the fact that the employer chooses the plan administrator and sometimes even the investment selection. There is no guarantee the employer did enough homework and due diligence to select the best administrator with the lowest fees or a menu of investment choices broad enough to serve all the participating employees.

At retirement, employees have the option of continuing to keep their money in a tax shelter—it's called a Rollover IRA—and withdrawing their money gradually in their leisure years.

Another consideration here when looking for tax-deferred vehicles, which include 401(k)s and IRAs alike, is that tax-deferred doesn't mean tax-free. When taking money from these accounts, taxes will still be due.

Your 401(k) and IRA aren't the only vehicles with taxes baked into them. Do you realize that your monthly Social Security check will also be subject to taxes on up to 85% of that benefit? How about capital gains taxes on your regular investments? Pensions are also subject to income taxes.

All that taxation of your accounts represents a threat to your assets, siphoning away value from your finances year after year. Each nickel you pay out in taxes is a dime that you have to put in the top of your financial bucket early on if you want to be able to take out a sufficient income someday. Put this way, can you see how one of the most advantageous things you can do for your financial situation is to have a coordinated plan of attack for your taxes?

Cutting down on taxes and taking a smart approach to minimize the drain can mean the difference in thousands of dollars a year for your retirement income.

Frank: Breaking Up Is The Right Thing To Do

As you approach retirement, it is a great time to examine how your current firm is doing and whether they are managing your plan well enough to ensure efficiency and security for your current and future needs.

Consider the story of Frank, a successful attorney, who spent twenty years with a well-known legal firm. He was fortunate to have no-cost access to a financial planner as a fringe benefit.

Such long relationships between clients and investment firms are not unusual. About 75% of clients have been with their financial professionals for ten or more years. Should the need to change course and advisors arise, a long relationship makes breaking up even tougher.

Yet Frank had a nagging feeling that the relationship with his current advisor might not be as beneficial as it could and should be. While the company maintained a relationship with the same firm over the years, the current representative assigned to Frank lived in a different state and only occasionally came out to Las Vegas for account reviews.

With Frank's retirement quickly approaching, the strategy for his personal plan had not been updated. Much of his retirement money was in his company sponsored 401(k) which had limited investment selections and above-average fees. His advisor had talked a bit about Social Security and that he should consider drawing from it while allowing his retirement assets to grow, but he hadn't mentioned anything about the tax implications when Frank turned 70 ½ and government-mandated required minimum distributions kick in.

For those who are not familiar, IRAs, 401(k)s, and other similar accounts have required minimum distributions, or RMDs. Based on a government-determined schedule of your life expectancy, you need to withdraw a specified percentage of certain tax-deferred accounts—and pay the appropriate income tax on the distribution. Failure to do so comes with a fine of up to 50% of whatever your missed RMD was. When we're talking about accounts that can hold hundreds of thousands of dollars, the tax implications are significant to say the least. The larger a tax-deferred retirement account grows, the more its owner will pay in taxes. It's like a tax bomb that only gets bigger with time.

CHAPTER SEVEN: TAX PLANNING

Frank got it—some portion of his savings needed to be in low-risk assets. He did not want to take a big hit to his assets and potentially outlive his income in the case of an economic meltdown, and he definitely didn't want to have his hard earned retirement assets eroded by poor tax planning.

Leaving a financial advisor is a bit like breaking up with a boyfriend or girlfriend. It's not easy or fun, but sometimes it needs to be done. It's these occasions where you need to make a business decision with your head, not your heart. There is too much at stake to allow emotions or sentiment to cloud your judgement.

A Cornerstone Retirement Blueprint emphasizes a comprehensive approach because a situation like Frank's is about much more than just taking income from Social Security and his 401(k). It's also about how those two income sources will be taxed and work together, both now and in the future, and how to generate the most reliable outcome possible for Frank.

Priscilla and Dwayne: Cruising Through Retirement

Some wouldn't describe how this next couple spends their days as work. See what you think.

Dwayne, 84, and Priscilla, 83, retired as schoolteachers but they never quit "working." As a couple they spend much of the year traveling around the world teaching bridge. A cruise here, a hotel seminar there, another cruise… their work takes them to exotic lands and gives their lives meaning and purpose.

Dwayne and Priscilla have their home base in a quiet, Las Vegas retirement community. Because they are away so much, their grandchildren often come to town and stay there. They love being in the position where they can spend time and money on those who matter the most. They also willingly take on other financial responsibilities such as caring for a son-in-law who is hospitalized and unable to work and helping to pay for family weddings and vacations. Who says grandparents have to stop spoiling the kids?

Typically, teaching is not the most lucrative of professions—at least not in the financial sense, but Priscilla and Dwayne finished their first careers with a combined $1.3 million in savings. They grew up in an era where saving was prioritized over spending and their money was very important to them because they didn't come by it easily.

As often is the case, the couple's nest egg was not receiving the necessary attention it should have been. Before coming to Cornerstone, they had been with a large "wirehouse" firm and had been frustrated by the fact that whenever they had a question or needed some service on the account, they were bounced around to different departments and representatives. There was no personal touch or access to a specific account manager. In the later years of that relationship, their portfolio returns were mediocre at best, but it was difficult to determine actual returns because they were buried in statements that could be 40 pages or more.

They had attended a dinner seminar and met a financial advisor who convinced them to sign some paperwork that, as they understood it, would give him access to financial information about their accounts. In reality, the forms were used to transfer their assets to a new account in their name at his firm.

They signed, but something did not sit right with Priscilla. They had met him at a dinner seminar, but their second visit was at their home. Why not at his office? Did he even have an office? When they returned from a cruise, they learned that their money was already in the process of being transferred. They asked Cornerstone for guidance and help.

It would take four meetings with them to unravel the mess and plot a course correction. Buried in the 40-page statements from the initial large financial institution was that it was charging the couple $27,000 a year in fees. Over one four-year stretch, their account had actually declined because there was not enough growth to overcome the fees.

We also discovered some things about the new firm, where the assets were to be transferred, that made us feel uncomfortable as well. The firm's principals were not financial planners or registered representatives with FINRA (the Financial Industry Regulatory Authority). They only had a license to sell insurance-based products.

In this case, transferring all of their assets at once had triggered large fees and generated significant income taxes.

Given the couple's age and lifestyle, the various entities that had handled their affairs hadn't given them enough liquidity, and acted negligently when it came to managing taxes and fees. These negative forces served as a headwind for growth and drained their portfolio unnecessarily. Not all fees are bad, and yes, ofttimes it's true that "you get what you pay for". The financial services world is no different. Yet, you should feel that you're getting value for your fees, and in this case Priscilla and Dwayne were essentially paying for poor performance…in more ways than one.

SUMMARY

Taxes and fees can have an unnecessarily negative impact on your portfolio, but with the right planning, you can avoid paying exorbitant fees and more taxes than your patriotic (and legal) duty demands.

Chapter Seven: Tax Planning

Jerry and Roberta: Making Retirement Plans Early

People from all walks of life and at all points on the earnings spectrum come through the front door of Cornerstone Wealth Management. Some feel like they are in a Catch 22, that the rules and tools we use won't work in their case and that no financial product can meet their needs. Sometimes they learn, after considerable discussion and research by their advisor, that the perfect solution does indeed exist in an investment vehicle they didn't even know about. So was the case with Jerry and Roberta, both were high earners in their respective careers. Jerry, a loan officer and Roberta, a real estate agent.

Jerry was the consummate overachiever. Work was his life; leisure time and hobbies always took a backseat. He made considerable contributions to the community on his own, producing two hours of radio shows a week to educate consumers on real estate and loan topics.

Like Jerry, Roberta was in her late thirties when they first came to Cornerstone.

Jerry received W-2 earnings as an employee but was not offered a 401(k)-retirement plan. Even if the company did have a qualified plan in place, that would not have helped Jerry and Roberta save as much as they'd like since the annual salary deferral contributions into a 401(k) plan were capped at $19,000 at the time.

Jerry consistently made $500,000 to $700,000 a year and wanted to set a large portion of that money aside for his retirement years. He was not trying to put off paying the tax man. In fact, he would rather pay taxes on income received during his high-earning years and at a time of historically low taxes, than when he retired and had only Social Security and the yield on his personal savings.

Jerry's employment status means that many tax-sheltered vehicles were not available to him, or not to the extent that would provide him the help he needs.

401(k)? No, because the annual contribution limit—$19,000 in 2019—was far less than Jerry would like to set aside during real estate boom years. There also were some salary phaseout limits…and his company didn't offer one anyway.

Roth IRA? This vehicle, where contributions are taxed up front but grow tax-deferred, with withdrawals not taxed at all, has a salary limit or phase-out. For married couples, it was $203,000 in 2019.

SEP or Simplified Employee Pension? This is a plan for business owners or the self-employed. Jerry was an employee so he could forget about contributing up to an effective limit of 20% of his earnings to a maximum of $54,000 annually.

IRA or Individual Retirement Account? There was a contribution limit of $6,000 a year for someone his age and he would not get the tax deduction because it starts to phase out for couples when they earn more than $103,000.

You get the picture. There was no obvious financial product that corresponded to what Jerry was trying to accomplish.

The question you're probably asking is: How can someone make a mid-six figure income year after year as an employee? Because he's really good at what he does, and he worked a lot.

Jerry hadn't had a day off in nearly two years. On his scheduled days off, you normally could find him in the radio room recording live shows. These programs helped his business, but they also performed a public service by educating consumers on topics like the real estate market, what kind of loan options are available, and credit repair.

Despite recent downturns in real estate (2008 for example), Jerry's income had been consistent. But both he and Roberta's incomes were tied to the real estate industry, and they were aware that even a mild cyclical downturn could be spawned by a rise in interest rates, a drop in consumer confidence, or tightened lending standards.

What they wanted was a retirement savings vehicle that was flexible so they could plan a schedule of projected annual savings, but if the economy changed, they could adjust that figure as needed.

Jerry and Roberta were somewhat concerned about the volatility of the stock market. Real estate was an alternative investment but they already owned some investment properties and Cornerstone was quick to point out that if the real estate market collapsed the couple would take a double hit. The value of their holdings would drop at the same time their income from their real estate centered careers suffered.

One possibility for someone in Jerry and Roberta's situation is an index universal life insurance policy, or IUL. Like any insurance policy, there's a death benefit, but if structured and funded correctly you can take tax-free loans from the contract.

There is no guaranteed income or return with Index Universal Life. However, the policy is tied to a stock market index, such as the Standard & Poor's 500, allowing for potential gains. Usually there is a cap on the gain a contract holder can participate in during a given time period—sometimes up to 12%—but if the market goes down, the contract owner is protected and does not lose any of their principal or gains. Again, this means that if funded correctly, after a certain amount of years it's possible that the gains will be enough to keep the policy in force without additional premium payments and may even provide an alternative source of income in retirement.

Since this strategy uses after-tax money to fund the policy, it means they will not have to pay any taxes on money taken out later for income purposes. Subsequently, this income stream will not affect their Social Security tax levels.

Index Universal Life has other positive features. If the individual should die prematurely, the premium paid into the contract blossoms into a tax-free death benefit for their beneficiaries. Depending on the insured's age, health status, needs and funding levels of the contract, this death benefit can be in the millions of dollars. As icing on the cake, many IUL policies also have long-term care components built-in or as a rider.

Most people who seek advice from a financial advisor don't have "indexed universal life insurance" on their mind or even in their vocabulary. That's fine. But it pays to have a financial professional on your team who can provide outside-the-box guidance for planning a tax-efficient retirement and solving other financial needs.

SUMMARY

Work with a financial professional who understands tax strategies and can execute them in conjunction with a tax professional.

Be sure all pieces of your plan are working together to be as tax and fee efficient as possible.

CHAPTER EIGHT

Health care planning

When Tragedy Strikes

If you have a solid income strategy, a tax-efficient portfolio and your investments are working away building up in your accounts, you're on the path to a carefree retirement... at least financially speaking! Yet, one of the biggest threats to a well-planned retirement is a prolonged illness or medical emergency. It's like the longtime Las Vegas resident and former heavyweight champion of the world, Mike Tyson said. "Everyone has a plan until they get punched in the mouth..."

An unexpected illness, accident, or medical condition can punch you and your best laid financial plans right in the mouth. To protect your plans and accounts for such events, long-term health care gets its own section in the Cornerstone Retirement Blueprint. We treat it this way because it is so important and potentially devastating. Events requiring long-term care are more common than you might think. According to LongTermCare.gov, 7 out of 10 Americans over age sixty-five will need some form of long-term care in their life. Yet, there aren't many truly good ways to address this legitimate concern.

Sure, there's your traditional long-term care insurance contracts. But those can be expensive and have drawbacks. If you know you will need it someday (i.e., have been diagnosed with a significant medical issue or have had a health event that may require long-term care), you most likely won't qualify for a new policy. And if you already have one but never use it, all those years of expensive premiums will be gone with nothing to show for it. Use it or lose it!

One option is you can self-fund your care. That said, the national average for long-term care is approaching $80,000 a year, and that's just for a semi-private room. $80,000 a year is a lot to fund out of pocket, especially if you end up needing multiple years of care.

You also have the government option, Medicaid, as a potential solution. Yet, as you may know, to qualify for Medicaid, you basically need to be a pauper in the eyes of the state. Meaning, you first must spend down your own assets to reach the level of impoverishment before the state steps in

Chapter Eight: Health care planning

to "take care of you." And by doing this, you sacrifice control of your circumstances, delegating to the state decisions about where you will live and what type and quality of care you will receive.

Neither of those alternatives are what we would consider strategic funding options. Yet, failure to plan for health care in your later years can wreak havoc on an otherwise-well-planned retirement strategy.

Now, there are a few other options available that can help. Fixed and fixed index annuities, which we've touched on before, are products where you put your money with an insurance company and defer taking income from it so that the contract value can grow modestly at a fixed or variable rate. Most index annuities have internal options called "riders" available for free or for an additional fee. These riders allow you to enhance the policy benefits in case of a long-term care incident. We've seen several policies that have "long-term care doublers," meaning that, once a policyholder has entered long-term care and meets certain criteria, the annuity company will actually double its contractual payout rate for 2 or sometimes even 3 year period. That said, even this solution comes with caveats that need to be considered before implementing it in your plan. Yet sometimes they can be a superior option over a use-it-or-lose-it, traditional long-term care policy.

All the above-described options fall somewhat short in today's high-cost health era. They're designed to supplement the costs associated with long-term care, not necessarily cover them in entirety. But let's be reminded of the statistic mentioned earlier that 70% of us will require some kind of long-term care. Not having a plan in place is not a viable option if you'd like to leave behind a legacy or are uncertain if your retirement assets are sufficient.

In conjunction with all the other financial concerns one might have, a health care event can take a huge emotional toll, both on the person whose health is suffering, as well as their spouse or other familial caregivers. Traumatized with worries and thrown into huge new responsibilities without preparation, a spouse tends to be overwhelmed. Overnight, there can be major role reversals and that nagging worry of facing financial ruin because of huge medical bills weighs heavily, destroying peace of mind.

Harry and Sally: Changing Roles

The names here are as fictional as the Hollywood romantic comedy. In fact, that was the impression the couple made when they first showed up at Cornerstone: like someone walking off a 1950s movie set.

This was a couple with the traditional division of household responsibilities. The husband always handled the

Chapter Eight: Health care planning

financial affairs and planning. The wife tended to the domestic side. While Sally was present at financial consultations, it was Harry who did most of the talking and who made the final decision.

The couple had no kids; they did have each other. Theirs was a story of romance and of fun-loving times that included dancing the night away and hosting fabulous, themed parties.

All this was before "the call."

It was just before Harry's 70th birthday, always a doubly fun event because his birthday falls on the 4th of July. Sally called us from the emergency room, saying Harry had suffered a severe stroke. She was in shock, concerned for her husband, and left worried and wondering, "What am I going to do?"

Although Sally had always accompanied Harry for the office visits, she was usually the silent partner. Now, she needed to take control, yet she was overwhelmed.

A monster medical crisis had emerged from the dark – unpredictable and devastating in its appearance. It always seems to happen to someone else, but we seldom consider that it might happen to us.

The fallout from a medical crisis or tragedy is bad because often it comes suddenly, without warning. Many are unprepared to handle the responsibilities that come with caring for a loved one who becomes disabled, bedridden, or is suffering from a debilitating mental illness. Although our instincts might pressure us to simply put our heads in the sand and hope the problem goes away, we cannot just run away and hide.

Back to Harry and Sally. First things first. The medical professionals would take care of Harry. Still, arrangements had to be made to transfer him to a short-term care facility and eventually to a long-term rehabilitation center.

Steps had to be taken to stave off the financial bleeding. Rehabilitation care can be expensive: costing more than $200,000 annually at many facilities.

Sally was panicked that the medical and care facility expenses would exhaust their life savings. She knew that Harry could be under short-term care for up to six months—something not covered under traditional long-term care policies. But she took comfort in knowing that the couple had a net worth of about $2 million and did have some long-term care insurance.

Harry was confined to a $600-a-day "short-term" care facility, and the long-term care insurance wouldn't kick in for six months. Liquidity becomes very important during this sensitive time. Withdrawals from any tax-sheltered accounts

Chapter Eight: Health care planning

had to be carefully planned as they would be treated as a taxable event. For example, if $100,000 was needed for care expenses, $140,000 might have to be withdrawn to take care of the taxes.

Below is a break-down of some of the needs Sally and Harry were facing:

- Liquidity to cover immediate needs
- Asset protection to ensure Harry's diminished health didn't adversely affect Sally's lifestyle
- Tax planning to prevent their immediate liquidity requirements from incurring unneeded tax burdens

Underscoring all of this was the aforementioned reality that Sally's role in handling the finances over the past several decades was passive. We see this frequently and have heard other advisors express this dynamic as "The Financial Alpha." The Financial Alpha could be either the husband or the wife; regardless, they are the ones who typically crunch the numbers and take an active role in financial decision-making.

There's nothing wrong with having a Financial Alpha in a relationship. But a health care event can turn this dynamic on its head.

One couple we know of, we'll call them Jack and Diane, were a perfect embodiment of this. Diane was the Financial Alpha—she had been a stay-at-home mom, math tutor, and piano teacher, and had run the family finances like a well-oiled machine, balancing the checkbook down to the exact penny. Jack was a musician, and somewhat of a dreamer. In one meeting, Diane was outlining goals and financial strategies, and she suddenly turned and looked at Jack, saying, "What does he need to know if something happens to me, or if I die first?" That got Jack's attention, for sure. The thought of something happening to Diane hadn't really occurred to him—after all, men typically predecease their wives. She gently reminded him that his own grandfather had spent a decade caring for his wife due to early-onset dementia. The look on Jack's face was priceless as he considered the possibility of taking over the couple's finances. He sat up a little straighter and made a noticeable effort to be more involved in their financial meetings.

Since we know the couple, it made for a rather humorous scene, but it gets at the heart of one important aspect of long-term health discussions. Whether it's a long-term care event or premature death, is the Financial Beta prepared to become the Financial Alpha if necessary? To help assuage any asymmetrical financial knowledge and comfort level between spouses, Cornerstone has several events—nights out, dances, and other soirees—that are part fun, part educational. This way, the Financial Beta of a couple can fill in the blanks on their financial education without the pressure that sometimes comes from in-office meetings full of graphs, charts, numbers, and industry-specific jargon.

Now back to Harry and Sally. They were classic examples of a Financial Alpha and Beta, and Sally was faced with the daunting task of reversing their roles. The tasks of financial planning, asset protection, tax strategies, etc.—can be implemented by whatever qualified professionals are involved. Still, someone has to take the lead and actively make sure to coordinate, communicate, and advocate for both themselves and their partner who may be incapacitated. Thankfully, Sally was a quick learner. With our help she was able to get on top of all she needed to do as she transitioned over as the primary caregiver to her husband and as the CFO of her household.

Leonard and Patricia: Dealing With Sudden Tragedy

Leonard, 67 worked for a municipal water company and had retired five years earlier. Patricia, 68, had been a homemaker all her life, raising their now-grown son and daughter.

Leonard was active and incredibly healthy for his age. He was always outdoors and a loyal member of the local gun club where he enjoyed skeet shooting. He was clearly a solid rock in his family and loved by his wife and kids. No one foresaw the heart attack.

Patricia was left alone with the funeral preparations, and on top of that, she now had to navigate a labyrinth of complex financial decisions. Shortly after Leonard's funeral, she was referred to us by a friend and set up an appointment, subsequently moving all their accounts over to Cornerstone. Now, instead of enjoying her golden years with Leonard, she was facing potential decades of retirement alone. She would, of course, lose the lower of the monthly Social Security checks, as well as being placed in a higher tax bracket. This is a common scenario that many are unprepared for following the death of a spouse: your tax deduction decreases, your Social Security and maybe your pension check decreases, but most of your expenses do not. Your utility bills don't go down by much. Your grocery shopping isn't majorly affected. Mortgage payments, if any, don't just magically disappear. Lower income and fewer deductions without a proportionate decrease in living expenses usually equate to a change in lifestyle.

After the new normal set in, Patricia mentioned to us that now her biggest priority was to leave a legacy for her kids. This came as no surprise: statistically, women are more inclined to leave a legacy than men. In order to make this happen, we would need to address the possibility of long-term care for Patricia.

In general, women are more likely to need long-term care than men, and typically for a longer period. One reason is that statistically women live longer—longer lives translate to more care down the road. Also, in our society, husbands tend to be older than their wives, and this amplifies the disparities between life expectancies. From an actuarial perspective, most men die married and most women die single; wives outlive their husbands more often than not. What does this all mean? Well, women end up taking care of their spouses as they age, and then their spouse passes away, leaving fewer options for someone to care for the widow as she ages.

We're not bringing these points up to scare you. It's just to emphasize why this is such an important piece of the Cornerstone Retirement Blueprint. Without taking the time to figure out a strategy for long-term health care coverage, someone in Patricia's circumstances may not be able to leave the legacy they want for their children and grandchildren.

No one wants to spend time dwelling on what might happen when they are suffering through the death or prolonged illness of a loved one. But the reality is, thinking this through and planning now for the "what-ifs" in life will enable you to make rational decisions, free from the emotions and stress of having to make those decisions when the pressure is on. Planning ahead gives you freedom to live your life before tragedy strikes, the freedom of options and to make your own decisions in case it does.

SUMMARY

Think through your wants and needs for health care, both in the immediate future and in the event of a long-term care event.

Discuss what the Financial Beta may need in case the Financial Alpha is incapacitated.

If married, plan for potential changes to your lifestyle and financial circumstances in the event that a Social Security or pension benefit decreases and your income tax increases after the death of a spouse.

Also, consider your wants for later age—is it your preference to stay in your home as long as possible? Will your current living situation need any adjustments for you to age in place? Consider the cost of installing wheelchair ramps, stairlifts, etc.

CHAPTER NINE

Legacy Planning

Reading through the stages of the Cornerstone Retirement Blueprint may seem overwhelming. From the daily activities of a good day in retirement to the tougher questions of what to do if you or your spouse are affected by dementia or another long-term care situation... there's a lot to process and plan for. Take heart! At Cornerstone, we don't work this out with you in one day. Addressing these major life questions is a process that we take one step at a time, and that we try to make as relaxed as possible.

Legacy planning is the final step of the Cornerstone Retirement Blueprint, but it isn't the least of the pieces by any means. No matter how much money you have to work with or what your goals are in regard to your legacy, this crucial component must work seamlessly in conjunction with all the other parts. For instance, it would be foolish to think that you can avoid tax reduction strategies for your estate and qualified accounts, or plan for long-term care expenses and still expect to leave your beneficiaries a sizeable inheritance. Conversely, if your idea of a legacy and quality of life in retirement is spending time with those you care about (rather than passing on your assets), then spending hours away at a soul-sucking job to acquire more reserves may not be the best way to use your time.

We work with experienced, qualified estate planning attorneys to ensure your assets are aligned with your legacy goals and that they follow the optimal, legal means for transfer to your beneficiaries in the most tax-efficient manner possible.

We have seen all kinds here at Cornerstone. Some sacrifice and save every penny they can for the generation to come. Others are more concerned with using their assets while they are alive to enjoy their retirement, saying they want the very last check they write to bounce.

An old Japanese proverb says, "There are many paths to the top of Mount Fuji." Likewise, there are many paths to and through retirement. Aside from major financial and estate planning mistakes, there are no right or wrong answers here. It all comes down to personal preference.

Chapter Nine: Legacy Planning

We'd like to share a few more stories about some of the situations we've encountered and assisted with over the years, and perhaps you will recognize one that is similar to your own. The takeaway in all of these is obvious: no matter your preferred legacy, planning ahead will help you achieve the impact you desire.

Harold and Leilani: Making Money Last

What if your retirement funds need to last a very long time, say 52.9 years?

Many couples preparing for retirement realize that one of them could easily live twenty years after working and the other even longer. There is a legitimate fear of outliving their money and anxiety about what to do about that possibility.

Other couples must make their money last even decades longer, such as parents who have a child with special needs. They strive to leave an endowment to provide financial support or care for someone who cannot make it entirely on their own.

That's often the case in May-September romances like Harold and Leilani's.

Harold was 69, and Leilani, his wife, was 29.

Harold's life was in transition. He was a nuclear engineer who had just retired, although a major university in northern

California was about to hire him as a consultant. They were transitioning from living in Silicon Valley to a suburb of San Diego in the extreme southern part of the state. After selling their home up north, they threw themselves into the herculean task of refurbishing the older house near San Diego. Harold had bought the home about eight years earlier in anticipation of retirement. After marriage Leilani had trained in the culinary industry as a chef. Harold wanted to leave her a financial legacy to augment any employment income. One more important factor in all this was Harold's adult, autistic son from his first marriage; Harold being the sole provider for him since his wife passed away many years earlier.

The portfolio Harold brought to the table needed more refurbishing and overhaul than their San Diego home. Harold wanted to leave as much as he could to his wife, who, according to actuarial tables, could live another 52.9 years. Before retiring, Harold had been more concerned about preserving his wealth rather than chasing returns. Now, in a new life stage, he recognized the danger that, if changes weren't made, Leilani would likely outlive their money. And what would happen to his son should the coffers run dry?

Harold's $1.3 million-dollar portfolio when he came to Cornerstone was 60% in cash. The other 40% was invested in the market. Why so much cash? Harold had gotten spooked

Chapter Nine: Legacy Planning

in 2012, expecting a market downturn and pulled money out. He tried to time the market, waiting for a good time to put the money back in, but he never made the move.

That's a common mistake: people panic in a downturn and move their investments to cash instead of riding the market out. Then, when the market morphs back from a "bear" to a "bull," their money remains on the sidelines. They miss out on a great growth opportunity for their investments.

Harold figured they needed an additional $70,000 a year on top of Social Security and miscellaneous income to live comfortably in California. That was not likely to happen with over three quarters of a million dollars sitting on the sidelines.

Clearly, with a career in nuclear energy behind him, Harold was a capable and intelligent man. He realized that when it came to building a financial strategy that must last not just for one, but two lifetimes, he didn't want to go it alone.

For those in a situation such as Harold and Leilani's, numerous factors are relevant in their overall Cornerstone Retirement Blueprint, but particularly to their legacy strategy component. For starters, when you have such a difference in age, the chances of one spouse outliving the other by decades is very likely. Another consideration is that with couples of disparate ages, it's not uncommon that at least one of them was previously married, and they may have children for whom they want to leave a legacy. Given the youth of the other spouse, there is also the chance that the couple will have more children in the course of their marriage. There are many moving parts and possibly conflicting objectives which all come into play when developing an overall legacy plan. "How do we…

> …create a legacy that cares for the surviving spouse?"
>
> …create an endowment for Harold's special needs son?"
>
> …create a legacy that provides for other children from any past relationships?"
>
> …create a legacy that provides for any children who may result from this union?"

As mentioned above, sometimes these interests are in competition—even in a situation where all parties care deeply about each other, it's possible that a planning misstep can result in people being left out and hurt feelings that can last decades or even a lifetime.

Fortunately, we were able to help Harold and Leilani restructure their investments, providing the proper amount of income to support their family after Harold retired. We were even able to carve out enough income to purchase an insurance policy on Harold's life, which proceeds would fund a special needs trust for his son upon Harold's passing.

Wills, Trusts and Beneficiaries

We have seen wills that accidentally disinherited children from a current marriage, or from a previous one. We've seen estate planning (or lack thereof) where children from a previous marriage inherited the house and, in a move that would have shocked their deceased mother, gave her surviving husband a mere month's notice to relocate from his residence of twenty years. In one trust review we did with a client, he was surprised and dismayed to find out that his ex-wife, whom he divorced five years prior, was still the primary beneficiary of his entire estate.

It's not just about documents such as wills and trusts, however. Both can be trumped by beneficiary lines on life insurance, 401(k) policies, etc. Failing to keep these instruments up to date can have severe unintended consequences. One woman, we'll call her Anne, came in to see us after having built up a significant amount in her 401(k) at work. She had started her career as an administrative assistant for a pharmaceutical company when she was young and newlywed. After an abusive marriage, she filed for divorce. She continued working while going to school at night where she met Tony, the man of her dreams. They married and eventually adopted three children. Tony supported her as she climbed her way up the corporate ladder to an executive position, complete with a corner office. When we met Anne, she was dressed impeccably, hair perfectly coiffed, and had a very professional manner; clearly, a woman who liked to keep her ducks in a row. She told us over coffee about the recent, tragic loss of her husband, Tony, and through gracious tears, she described the life they had built. She showed us pictures of their children and grandchildren—a grandson who was a competitive viola player, a granddaughter who was a dual major in art and business. At a subsequent meeting, she was shocked when we reviewed her 401(k) that she had long invested in, and there on the beneficiary line: Eric. Her ex-husband.

If she had died without changing the beneficiary, hundreds of thousands of dollars would have gone to him instead of providing the legacy she dreamed of for her grandchildren.

We share these experiences to make the point: legacy planning isn't a "set it and forget it" event. Updating your plans and strategies as your life changes is a must.

You are likely familiar with the legacy planning document of a will. This is adequate for some—a simple document that stipulates what you want to go where. Wills, however, must

Chapter Nine: Legacy Planning

go through probate—the court system for determining that a will is valid, identifies and inventories the deceased person's property, and then oversees that the will is executed correctly, and the assets are distributed appropriately.

As we've discussed, beneficiary lines can take precedence over what's dictated in a will, so it is particularly important to keep these up to date.

As far as trusts go, there are different kinds of trusts, such as revocable, irrevocable, marital, dynasty, asset protection, special needs trusts, etc. The specific focuses and functions of the various types of trusts available are beyond the scope of our book. Broadly, a trust is a legal device that gives you more control of whatever you title to it. You can stipulate how you'd like to divide the assets, and even put parameters around inheritance, such as mandating a beneficiary of the trust graduate college before gaining access, or doling out specific amounts as the beneficiaries reach ages or milestones in life. This can be especially helpful when you intend to leave your estate to multiple beneficiaries across different generations.

A caveat on trusts is that they only apply to whatever is titled to them. Therefore, if your cars, house, insurance, etc. are all titled to individuals, those titles will override the directives of your wills and trusts. So, be sure you write the name of the trust as the beneficiary or owner on any assets you wish to place in the trust.

Robert and Amanda: Compounding A Tragedy

Robert was a school administrator with about 35 years of experience. His wife, Amanda, was a teacher. Robert was in his mid-fifties, in good health, and wanted to retire young. Amanda wanted to continue teaching.

They asked us to assist them with some decisions relating to their pension planning. The district had presented Robert with three options, and he wanted to know the pros and cons of each.

Option one would present Robert with a monthly check of about $8,000. If he passed away, there would be nothing for Amanda.

With option two, Robert's monthly amount would reduce to about $6,500, and Amanda would continue to receive the same amount if he died first.

The third option would provide Robert with a monthly check of $7,250 a month. In the event of his death, that amount would be cut in half and continue for the remainder of Amanda's life.

The options are fairly standard in organizations that still offer traditional pensions. Option one provides the highest

Chapter Nine: Legacy Planning

monthly payout. However, it puts the survivor at grave risk of having an impoverished future. Option two takes care of the survivor, but the couple sees the initial retirement benefit lowered significantly. Option three cuts the survivor benefit in half, but as we mentioned earlier, not all expenses—home maintenance, utilities, car payments—drop by half with the death of a partner or spouse.

What many about-to-be retirees don't realize is that the mathematics of many standard pension options—meant to be one size fits all—favor the organization and the future of its pension program. They don't prioritize the needs of the retiree.

There's a pension alternative to this one-size-fits-all approach, though not everyone can qualify. It's built on a life insurance chassis, and we sometimes refer to it as a "pension maximizer." While preparing for their impending retirement, if the client is in good health and qualifies, they obtain an insurance policy with level premiums for up to twenty years, and the death benefit would provide a safety net against a lost pension benefit.

We explained that with the pension maximizer strategy, he could go with Option 1, taking the maximum monthly pension amount offered by his company, and then carve out $800 a month for the insurance premium. If Robert predeceased Amanda, his pension would stop; however, she would receive a check for $2 million, tax-free. So instead of "leaving $1,500 a month on the table," the monthly pension amount would only be reduced by $800, and Amanda would be financially secure should tragedy strike.

Robert had worked very hard all his life for this pension, and he considered it income that he was entitled to. Leaving $1,500 a month on the table (the difference between the no-survivor benefit option and the constant monthly check choice) didn't seem like a good strategy to him, so he and Amanda decided to choose option one, the $8,000 a month payment with no survivor benefit and they did not want to carve out the $800 a month for the life insurance premium. They simply wanted to maximize their monthly income in retirement and were not interested in the alternative strategies we presented.

The final bell rang for Robert as he left his career in school administration and entered the retired life. Later that same year, he and his wife took a trip to New York City for a little celebration. One evening, Robert decided to go down from the hotel to a restaurant across the street for coffee and some takeout. While crossing the street, he was hit and killed by a taxi.

Amanda had to face the harsh reality that not only did she lose her husband, but she also lost his retirement income.

Chapter Nine: Legacy Planning

After receiving only a few months of payments, the money that would have paid out for many years over Robert's retirement, remained in the pension fund for others, not Amanda. She faced a future of severe budgeting and working much longer than she anticipated. Her pension and retirement income would now be based on her work history alone, and all those years Robert had built up for his retirement, were for naught.

Robert never thought that he would get hit by a cab in New York City while celebrating his retirement with Amanda. Life is unpredictable, and one seldom anticipates tragedy when it comes. But you can protect and prepare yourself financially—put your fiscal house in order—and prevent compounding the tragedy if and when it comes.

That is what we strive to do at Cornerstone. We are more than a company that provides investment advice or health care solutions. We're planning for our clients' longevity, pension risk, estate preservation, and more. We want to help as many people as possible and prevent more tragic situations like what Amanda went through, from happening.

Russ and Frances: When Plans Go Right

It's easy, and frankly, kind of depressing, to just cherry-pick the cases of "doing it wrong" when it comes to legacy planning. Each year it seems a prominent celebrity dies without estate plans in place, leaving money to unintended beneficiaries such as the ex-spouse, estranged relatives, or Uncle Sam. From Michael Jackson to Joe Robbie, there are many high-profile cases of poor estate planning. It's inexcusable! Whether your estate is worth $100,000 or $100,000,000, plan today for a smooth and efficient transition tomorrow.

You'll always hear about when things go wrong. Bad news and the negative results of bad planning travel much faster and scream louder than the effects of good news and good planning. When your legacy plan goes right, there's usually not much to gossip about.

Russ and Frances were one such case. Both widowed, and both on their second marriage, they had three daughters between them—one was his, one was hers, and one they had together. Russ hadn't come into the marriage with much as far as material possessions. Frances, on the other hand, had a significant estate which she brought to the relationship. Together they raised their three girls as one family.

Prior to her death, Frances established multiple trusts to take care of her husband as well as all three of their daughters, and each trust had provisions unique to its respective beneficiary. During their marriage, Frances and Russ had multiple conversations over what equitable would look like, what her first husband would have wanted, and what was realistic for her and her daughters' current life circumstances.

Chapter Nine: Legacy Planning

Russ also put in place his own kind of planning in case he predeceased his wife. As their daughters reached adulthood, they included them in the conversation, explaining what the provisions were and why.

In the years following Frances' death, Russ revisited their legacy plans, and he too wrestled with the questions of equality, legacy, and love. When Russ passed, the three daughters, along with their spouses and children, all went to the funeral. They laughed, cried, and together revisited memories of their parents and the legacy they left behind. Although it was a sad time, because of the careful estate planning Russ and Frances had done while alive, there were no hard feelings, no one was left out or ostracized, and they were able to grieve and heal together as a family.

Juicy gossip about who inherited what, who was disinherited, and who won't ever show their face again at a family function may make for good daytime TV drama, but in real life, when a family member passes away, those factors can be emotionally and financially draining. The Cornerstone Retirement Blueprint aims to keep unnecessary drama out of the financial aspect of your retirement and create a "boring," dependable plan. The same goes for the legacy planning component. Because *how* you pass on your estate is just as much a part of the legacy as *how much* you pass on.

SUMMARY

Identify the goals for your legacy.

Find an estate planning attorney who will collaborate with the other members of your financial team.

If you have a spouse or partner, recognize what order you will need to leave things in should you predecease them.

Ask yourself what kind of legacy do you want to leave the next generation, financial and otherwise.

Ask what kind of a legacy you'd like to leave in the realm of charitable giving and causes you are passionate about.

Review if there are any family dynamics—children with special needs, or who children and grandchildren from previous marriages, just to name a few—that may require a more complex strategy.

Consider if there are estate and other tax implications that you should review in with your financial advisor and a CPA.

CHAPTER TEN

Choosing the Right Firm

The Cornerstone Retirement Blueprint is our process to:

1. Systematically and accurately account for your income in retirement.

2. Provide the potential for growth of your assets to keep up with or outpace the erosive forces of inflation.

3. Ensure that a significant health care event won't derail your plans.

4. Make certain your legacy is passed on the way you want.

5. Be sure all parts and pieces of this plan are implemented and coordinated to work at peak efficiency, minimizing taxes and fees while providing

for the requisite amount of secure, stable growth and income.

We are not the only financial firm that follows a system or plan to be sure all the bases are covered. There are many qualified advisors out there. We encourage you to seek out a financial professional who, at a minimum, follows a process and can provide comprehensive planning, because preparing for retirement is more than just accumulating a pile of money or investments and hoping you don't outlive your income.

Impersonal, cookie-cutter "invest and hope" strategies are one reason so many have an ingrained distrust of Wall Street and large financial institutions. Too many investors have been burned by improper planning or inappropriate investment advice. When searching for an advisor, think of it as a job interview where they are competing for the position to be your personal CFO. Get to know them and make sure they take the time to find out about you. By getting to know each other as individuals and not just part of a transactional interaction, we have a chance to build trust. We want clients to trust that Cornerstone will always give them sound, prudent financial advice. We want them to understand that when they come in to see us, they're not there to decide to hire us right away. In our initial meeting, we let them know upfront: "You're not making any decisions today. We're here to learn about each other, provide some information, and give you something to think about so you can take some time and make the decision that's right for you."

Cornerstone helps clients identify problems, gaps, or threats with their current financial situation and lets them know there are solutions. The client can then decide if, how, and when they want to move forward.

The reason we do so many educational events along with our radio show/podcast is that we are passionate about educating people about personal finance and sharing our experiences. Also, we want potential clients to get to know us personally. Just as we see our clients as individuals we know and care about, we want them to see us the same way.

When you are seeking out a financial professional, there are some guidelines and tests to determine whether it's a good fit. The following are just a few:

Finding the Right Advisor

Experience. There are a few things you want to know about an advisor before you enlist their services. One is how long they've been in the industry. We suggest this as a qualifier because the financial services industry has a high rate of burnout and turnover—you don't want to get started in planning retirement only to have your advisor leave in the middle of everything to become a cruise ship lounge singer (true story).

Focus. Not all areas of financial services are suitable for your life stage. As we discussed earlier, some financial professionals focus only on the accumulation part of finances. Others focus exclusively on employee benefits, like managing 401(k) retirement plans. Others still aren't registered representatives—someone who has their FINRA securities license(s)—and concentrate solely on strategies involving insurance products. Retirement planning demands a certain amount of specialization, but also a broad knowledge of many other strategies and products—insurance and investments alike—that can accomplish your specific retirement goals and objectives.

Education. There isn't just one standard for financial professionals. The term can cover a wide spectrum of experiences, certifications, and other qualifiers. One thing you want to look for is whether a person is licensed to discuss both insurance and investment based strategies. Also, consider that the financial industry is constantly changing, new products and strategies make older ones appear less efficient, even obsolete. Technology is pushing the bounds of what was once standard, creating "new normals" at a rapid pace. Asking your potential financial professional what

Chapter Ten: Choosing the Right Firm

licenses, designations, and qualifications they have and what continuing education they engage in is a must.

Communication. How will your financial professional's office contact you? How often will you hear from them, and from whom will you hear? If you need more frequent communication about your investments, or if you prefer to communicate via text messages instead of phone calls or vice versa, will the firm accommodate you? The advisor firm you choose needs to have communication procedures and capabilities that are firmly in line with your expectations, or else it is not a good fit.

Intuition. Sometimes the best indication of whether you should work with a person or firm has to do with your gut instincts. Some of the stories we shared throughout this book involved widowed clients who felt their former financial advisors didn't listen to them. During the initial meetings with your advisor, if you get the impression that you or your spouse/partner is being ignored, sold or talked down to—then make a "U" turn. It's one thing to be open to new information or innovative strategies; it's another to be venturing into financial or personal territory that makes you uncomfortable. Listen to your instincts, because a real relationship with your financial firm could be for the rest of your life, and you should be willing to take the time to get it right.

What Is A Fiduciary?

A critically important factor in choosing a retirement advisor is whether the individual is a fiduciary.

Fiduciary is more than a label or a definition; it is a standard of trust and obligation the advisor must meet where the clients' interests come first.

Prospective clients are asking the question more and more often, "Are you a fiduciary?" They realize that it can make a big difference in the amount of money paid out for advice and who benefits first from that advice—the advisor and sellers of financial products or the client. It can make a big difference as well, in the performance results of the client's portfolio.

The Employee Retirement Income Securities Act of 1974 has not been significantly revised since it was passed. In the ensuing decades, traditional pensions have gone the way of the dinosaur, and defined contribution plans like 401(k)s—which place retirement savings responsibility on the employee—have taken the place of the pension.

At Cornerstone, we insist that all our advisors act as fiduciaries, even though the federal government does not require it. A fiduciary does what is in the client's best interest all the time. They cannot sell a certain financial product just because that specific company pays them the largest

Chapter Ten: Choosing the Right Firm

commission. Stockbrokers work on a suitability standard. For example, a broker might advise you to invest $100,000 of your $500,000 savings in Google stock, and all they must prove is that the investment is "suitable." A fiduciary is required to go a step further and prove that such an investment, with all the considerations including the risk it carries, is in the client's **_best_** interest. That's a huge difference.

Remember: A fiduciary puts you—not the salesman, advisor, or their company—first.

At Cornerstone, sometimes we work on a fee basis, and, at other times, we recommend commissionable products. We don't put anybody entirely in the market, and we won't ever put anyone entirely in insurance products; we offer well-rounded, comprehensive financial planning, and all of our advisors act as fiduciaries.

We consider ourselves more than just money managers. Our years in financial services have made us conversant in estate and legacy planning. We know about taxes and health care costs, how to address inflation, and strategic ways to decrease expenses and increase income.

At the end of the day, being a fiduciary really does make a difference. Cornerstone advises prospective clients that, whether it is us or someone else, always work with a fiduciary if possible.

Based on our observations, the search for the right advisor has three phases:

1. **Discovery** – This is where you learn about the various advisors your interviewing, their firm, expertise, capabilities, etc., and they, in turn, learn about who you are and gain some understanding of your current financial situation.

2. **Comparison Shopping** – Compare and discuss the various pros and cons of each firm and/or advisor, taking into consideration fees, product availability, accessibility, experience, and the aforementioned intuition or gut feeling.

3. **The Decision** – After weighing all the factors, make a choice and move forward with it.

We think it's worth expanding on each of these steps further because when it comes to choosing a financial advisor, we recommend hiring slowly now so you won't have to fire quickly in the future.

Let's take a deeper dive into each step.

Discovery

An informed decision depends upon just that: information about you as an individual, information about your financial situation, and information about your goals for retirement.

Chapter Ten: Choosing the Right Firm

The discovery step is as much about getting acquainted with the advisor as it is learning about yourself. Sometimes in life, certain events and questions surprise us with the realization that we do not fully know ourselves. Early in our planning process, Cornerstone gives all prospective clients a quiz using proprietary software—called Riskalyze—to measure the individual's tolerance for risk. Some people who come in tell us that they're conservative, and they don't want to lose their money. But then when we look at their investment holdings, we realize the risk they are taking is not in alignment with the reward they are expecting.

The Riskalyze questionnaire rates clients with a score from 1 to 100—1 being most conservative (think US Treasuries) and 100 being the riskiest (think giving your money to Charles Ponzi and asking him to play baccarat on your behalf). Their score is a good indicator as to how much risk they are willing to take on. Maybe a prospective client ends up with a risk score of 45. Once we've found that number, we enter all their existing investment positions into the software. Each entry has its own Risk Score, which is all added up and weight-adjusted for a final portfolio score. Many times we see the client who has a personal risk score of 45 is living with a portfolio that has a score of 80. The relationship between these numbers is not in harmony and will eventually lead to disappointment.

The first thing Cornerstone does is educate a client on what investments they already own and whether they are appropriate for them with respect to their financial resources, time horizon, and their feelings about risk.

The education process goes into other aspects to prepare the prospective client. It is important that they understand their working career is an accumulation (savings) phase, but as they get close to retirement, they are about to enter a distribution (spending) phase, harvesting from their savings. We help them understand not just their investments and income but their expenses as well. If their expenses in retirement are high relative to their income, they tend to take unnecessary risks in order to achieve the necessary gains to sustain their lifestyle, and often wind up regretting it.

Comparison Shopping

Do you remember your last year of high school and the challenge of choosing what to do after graduation? Do you go to college? Big or small university? Live at home or cut the cord and get out on your own? Should you attend a public or private school, and how are you going to pay for it? Did you have to decide between a school that specializes in your desired field, or did you need time in the university environment just to figure out what you were interested in?

Chapter Ten: Choosing the Right Firm

Next, maybe came campus visits, touring the grounds, auditing a class, talking to a few faculty members and students.

Selecting a retirement advisor is similar in many ways to the process of deciding the course for your post-secondary education. At Cornerstone, we think that comparison shopping is a valuable exercise and suggest the following questions that can serve as yardsticks in making your decision:

- How often do you see clients? Are account reviews quarterly or annually? If my advisor is on vacation, who covers for him/her?

- How long has your firm been serving residents in the area? Are your staff locals in the community or transplants from out of town? What is their average length of service, and what's the turnover in your office?

- Are services you provide paid for by hourly fees, commission sales of products, or a hybrid combination? There are advantages and disadvantages to both systems, and you should understand that no one approach or product can fit every client's needs.

- Are you a fiduciary? Do you put the client first before the firm or yourself? Or must you only meet a suitability standard, a lesser requirement that may not be in my best interest?

- Who provides your advice on topics that are possibly outside your area of expertise such as taxes, Social Security, long-term care needs, trusts, estate planning, etc.?

- Are you experienced enough to help plan around my unique circumstances?

- Do you have account minimums in order to work with your firm? (The principal partners at Cornerstone have established account minimums, although associates can, and do, provide basic services for accounts that are smaller.)

- Finally, does it feel right? Can I picture myself on this campus, with this firm? If I walk into this financial office 6 months from now, will anybody even recognize me?

We hope that people will use Cornerstone as the benchmark for the comparison. We are transparent, upfront, and present our value proposition and, in confidence, let the other advisors and firms make their own case.

We believe in frequent reviews, continuing contact, and ongoing client education. We often joke and say we see our clients more than their kids do. In some cases, it's true.

Chapter Ten: Choosing the Right Firm

The Decision

Once you have solidified your relationship with a financial professional and have followed their process for establishing your retirement strategy, there is a final step where some trip up: executing on that plan.

It reminds us of something one of our clients, Donna, told us about her middle-school-aged grandson. He was a bright child and quite funny, who always made his grandmother laugh with his insights and unique perspectives.

Yet, his parents told Donna that he was frequently on the verge of failing in school, something teachers attributed to him not doing the homework. His grandmother couldn't believe it—during many of his visits, he diligently completed his homework assignments while she looked on, and he would even explain in detail what he was studying.

One day, Donna arrived to pick her grandson up from school for a weekend visit. She'd arrived early, so instead of waiting, she parked and went inside to find him. She walked him from his last class of the day to his locker, laughing as he told her funny stories from his day. As he opened his locker, she noticed wads of crushed paper at the bottom, a pile that threatened to fall out the longer his locker was open. As he went to shut the door, she stopped him and asked about the papers. He blushed and said they were just trash. Of course, in her grandmotherly way, Donna scooped some of the paper up and began to smooth them out. She soon realized that she had stumbled upon the missing homework assignments.

She gently confronted her grandson, more confused than upset. Ashamed, he explained that, despite spending hours researching and doing homework, he was afraid some of it was wrong. What if he'd answered incorrectly, or had misunderstood some of the questions? His pre-teenaged anxiety had convinced him it was better to not act for fear of being wrong, or of making a mistake.

Like the old sports adage, "you miss 100% of the shots you don't take," Donna's grandson was nearly failing his classes for fear of missing a few problems on the homework.

Similarly, we see people who have done the painstaking work of going through the process to plan their retirements. They like what they see on paper, but when it comes time to execute and implement the plan, they freeze. They would rather maintain the status quo, even if it doesn't suit their needs, simply because it is a known, familiar situation.

Don't let "analysis paralysis" keep you from taking the necessary steps toward your retirement dreams—you've worked hard through your life to accumulate enough money to retire, and now it's time to let your money work hard for you.

Chapter Ten: Choosing the Right Firm

Final Thoughts About Finding An Advisor

Clients who come to Cornerstone for an initial consultation take the computerized quiz, objectively matching their investment comfort level with the assets in their portfolio. During the getting-to-know-you sessions, our advisors review the clients' financial situation and strive to discover what will make them happiest and most comfortable in retirement.

Then, all Cornerstone advisors are trained to look for obvious flaws or threats in the clients' financial situation: portfolios mismatched to clients' investment comfort; "Lazy money" assets that won't produce enough income to meet their living expenses; risky portfolios that may be ravaged in a severe stock market downturn; overly conservative portfolios with little chance for growth; assets that may produce enough income now, but after ten years of inflation their purchase power has diminished; financial plans that have not factored in a legacy for the kids, the needs of a surviving spouse, or the couple's desire to give back through significant charitable donations.

There are numerous other flaws, threats, and weaknesses that may manifest during discovery. For example, clients with financial plans that assume unrealistically high rates of return are likely to be disappointed when reality plays out.

Cornerstone advisors identify these flaws and may suggest broad, general fix-it steps that will become more detailed if and as the relationship continues.

Still, let's not forget the good news that often flows from these introductory meetings. For couples nagged by "How much is enough for retirement?" or "Will I ever have enough to retire comfortably?" are often told that they have plenty. They can retire early, or they can continue to do the work they enjoy with one less thing to worry about.

We hope you will find value in the outlined approach for finding the right advisor and use it as a foundational base while doing your comparison shopping and making your choice.

SUMMARY

Find a financial advisor who can help you with the specific, unique needs that are appropriate for your stage of life

Establish trust and allow them to coordinate with the other members of your retirement team such as CPAs and attorneys

Execute your plan.

ACKNOWLEDGMENTS

A book is a massive undertaking and inevitably is a team project. We are grateful to one and all, even if their names do not appear here. Here is our shortlist:

- Henry DeVries. This self-described book doctor is that and much more. Henry is CEO and co-founder of Indie Books International and a prolific author. Henry's recent volume, "Marketing With a Book," served as a guide on our approach.

- Don Sevrens. A career journalist and lifelong investor, Don helped put our words on paper and was a vigilant gatekeeper to prevent financial jargon from slipping in.

- Kurt Hanson. His contribution to this book as a word-smith and storyteller has taken our book project to a higher level. We could not have gotten this book to print without him.

- Our clients. Much of this book is comprised of their stories. They put their trust in us, and things ultimately worked out well in the end. Our interactions started out as business relationships and quickly became much more. They are wonderful people, and it has been very satisfying and enjoyable helping them accomplish their goals while we build upon their financial and retirement plans. And it's been even more rewarding as we've developed deep friendships with many clients and their family members.

ABOUT THE AUTHORS

Jammie Avila's leadership the last 10 years at Cornerstone Wealth Management has helped grow assets to almost 400 million dollars. Jammie and the team look forward to accomplishing their long term goal of 1 Billion.

Jammie and his wife, Danielle, were married in 1999 and are the parents of four children. He enjoys playing golf, coaching his children in various sports, and traveling with his wife and family.

Kyle and his wife, Amanda were married in 1996 and have two children. He has enjoyed watching his daughter graduate college and become an elementary school teacher. He spent years helping coach his son who now excels in High School Sports.

Kyle's favorite motto is: "Never get so busy making a living that you forget to make a life."

The Cornerstone Retirement Blueprint Process

We believe our approach to retirement at Cornerstone is built on these major strengths:

- **Education.** Nobody cares more than we do about our clients' success. We make sure that they understand where they are headed by holding Client Education workshops. Knowledge is Power.

- **Experience.** Jammie, Kyle and all the members of the Cornerstone team have almost 100 years of combined experience.

- **Diversification.** We focus on using non-correlated assets in an endowment model approach. That's a fancy way of saying "don't put all your eggs in one basket" and have a plan designed to never touch the principal.

- **Being available.** Cornerstone is team-based with four main partners, associate advisors and an experienced staff all working together. If one of us is away, the others can pick up the phone and resolve any questions or issues.

- **Caring.** Our clients aren't numbers, like they are sometimes viewed as at the big wirehouses. Here, when you call, we know you by name and often by voice.

- **Continuity.** We're here today, we'll be here tomorrow. Many of our clients realize that we and our team will be able to help their kids when they retire.

A guiding principle for Cornerstone: Nobody wins by dying with the most amount of money. We win by not running out of money before we run out of life.

CONTACT US

We want you to get to know us, and hope we have the opportunity to meet you. This book augments and compliments our website https://cornerstonevegas.com/, weekly podcast, "The Cornerstone Retirement Blueprint," monthly public seminars, and personal interviews.

If you are ready to meet and find out if we are a good fit for you and your financial needs, please feel free to contact us at:

Phone: (702) 878-4742

Fax: (702) 878-4741

Email: info@cornerstonevegas.com

www.ingramcontent.com/pod-product-compliance
Lightning Source LLC
Chambersburg PA
CBHW071410210526
45465CB00001B/318